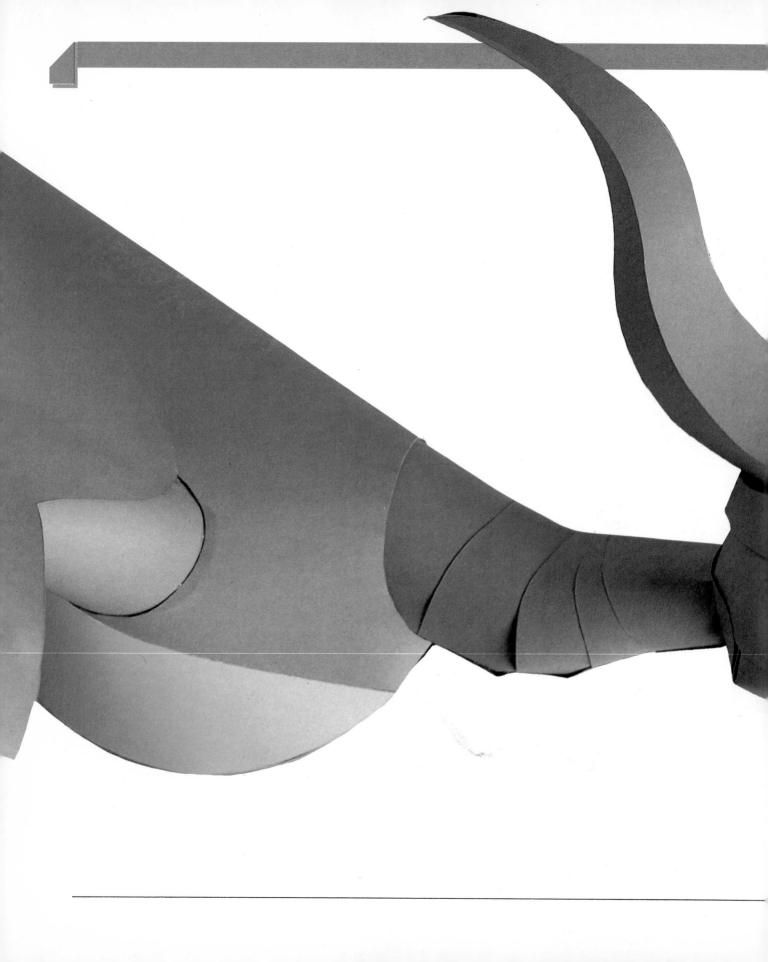

ART FROM PAPER

DAVID HAWCOCK

Crescent Books

New York

Editor: Donna Wood
Art Editor: Gordon Robertson
Photography: Alan Duns and Giles Johnson
Illustrations: John Hutchinson
Production: Richard Churchill

This 1987 edition published by Crescent Books, distributed by Crown Publishers, Inc., 225 Park Avenue South, New York, New York 10003.

© Marshall Cavendish Limited 1987

ISBN 0-517-64453-3

Typeset in 11/12pt Garamond by Bookworm Typesetting, 4 Sillavan Way, Manchester
Printed and bound in Italy by L.E.G.O. S.p.a. Vicenza

h g f e d c b a

For Rachel

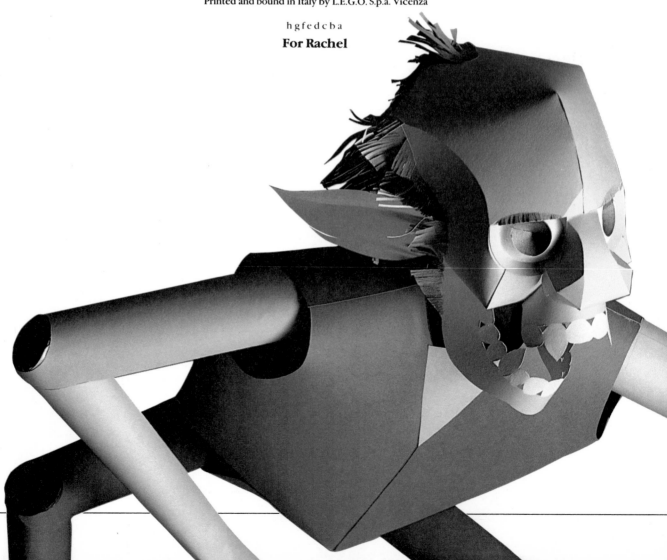

CONTENTS

POINTS TO REMEMBER ON EVERY PROJECT

■ Grey areas on the diagram are the areas where you should apply glue.

■ The scale of the model can be varied when you draw out the pieces.

■ Cut out large pieces with scissors and small pieces with a scalpel or craft knife.

■ Numbered parts join together, e.g. 1 will join to a second piece marked **1**. If the number is within a circle apply glue to the top of the piece, otherwise apply glue to the underside.

INTRODUCTION

Anyone who thinks that paper is white and oblong and made for writing letters has a few surprises in store. Think of the variety of paper to be found in the home. There is the soft tissue paper that comes in rolls and boxes and the thicker, more absorbent tissue used for wiping up spills in the kitchen. A kind of thick, fibrous paper is stuffed through the letterbox each morning with all the latest news printed on it. Much finer printed paper is found between the covers of expensive books. There is dull brown paper for packaging, shiny paper for presents, thick paper for cards and boxes, ultra-thin paper for tracing; wallpaper, flypaper, sandpaper, paper doileys and so on.

Paper is surely the most versatile material available to a modelmaker, and it has numerous other advantages. You don't need any expensive tools for working with paper, and nothing more specialized than simple watercolours or felt-tipped pens are needed to create the decoration you will see on the models in this book. The various other bits and pieces (such as adhesive tape and cotton) required for making all the models can be bought on any main street. Pilgrimages to specialized model shops are completely unnecessary when working with paper.

In Britain, weights are given as grammes per square metre (gsm or g/m^2). In the USA, lbs is the standard measurement and a basic conversion would be:

UK	USA
80 gsm	= Basis 25 × 38 in/54 lb
200 gsm	= Basis 20 × 26 in/74 lb
400 gsm	= Basis 20 × 26 in/148 lb

Grammes per square metre refers to the amount of paper needed to fill a square metre of area. So the more material laid, the thicker and stronger the paper. For example, 50 gsm would be the thickness of tissue, 400 gsm the thickness of a birthday card. Using the correct paper weight makes the model's life considerably longer. Attempts to make small, delicate shapes in thick card would not work, neither would cutting large, structural pieces from thin, flimsy paper. I have never made a conscious effort to learn about paper weights; experience and common sense is the key.

There is always an exception to the rule and this is metallic paper. Shiny metallic paper (gold, silver and bronze) often does not come in different weights, only in a very thin delicate sheet. This problem is overcome quickly and easily – simply glue the metallic paper on to another sheet of a specific weight.

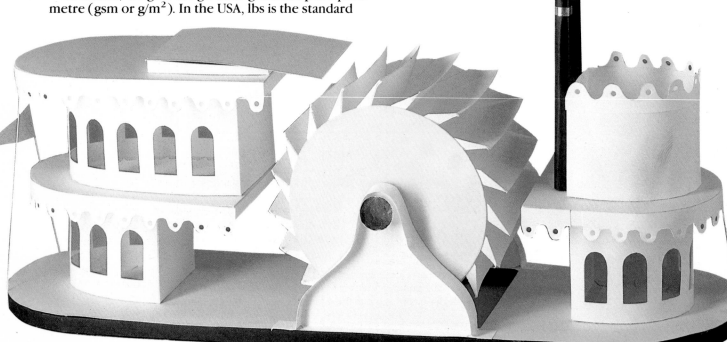

Paper Size Conversion Chart

Within this book, only four different sizes of paper in the ISO series have been used; SRA2, A2, A3 and A4. This chart provides a conversion table for metric and standard equivalents, to enable you to buy the right quantity of paper for each project:

	Metric	Standard
SRA2	450 × 640 mm	17¾ × 25¼ in
A2	420 × 594 mm	16½ × 23⅜ in
A3	297 × 420 mm	11¾ × 16½ in
A4	210 × 297 mm	8¼ × 11¾ in

Paper sizes provided by Wiggins Teape

Paper comes in a huge variety of sizes. In Britain paper used to come in odd sizes with fascinating names such as Elephant (23 × 28 in) or Large Post (16½ × 21 in) and of course Foolscap (13½ × 17 in). These have now been replaced by the ISO (International Standards Organisation) rectangular series. In this series A3 is half the area of A2 and double the area of A4. The proportion of height to width remains the same, regardless of size. Thus a diagram exactly filling A2 will also fit A1 or A7 if it is proportionally enlarged or reduced. The smaller the number, the larger the sheet of paper, so the largest in the series is A0, the smallest is A10. These paper sizes are easily available in Britain, but in the non-metric USA specific measurements for each sheet of paper will have to be given when buying paper.

There is a huge variety of coloured papers with many colour ranges. Each range varies slightly, so with some persistence the exact colour you require can usually be found. Some papers have flecks and colour variations that will add interest and character to any model. The imaginative paper sculptor can create huge variations in his or her work simply by choosing spectacular designs.

At the start of each project is a 'You will need …' box listing all the tools and materials necessary to complete each model. Scissors and a scalpel or craft knife are needed for all projects. The scissors (make sure they are really sharp) should be used to cut out all large pieces of paper; the scalpel or modelling knife is to make the more intricate cuts, *ie* any filigree work or small, curved shapes.

Instructions have been kept very simple, but several of the terms used throughout the book may need clarification here.

Scoring: The act of running the scalpel or knife blade across the paper, exerting enough pressure to make an indentation, but not enough to make a cut. This technique is often used along a line which is to become a fold in order to make it keep its shape.

Lining: On models with open mouths or visible interiors the inside of the model has been lined with paper of another colour (see the paddle steamer, or the goblin and Terror Dactyl with their glowing pink mouths for instance). Simply choose two pieces of paper, one for the interior and one for the exterior of your model, and stick them together, back to back. They can then be treated as one sheet, but on the finished model the inside colour will be visible whenever the outside is cut away.

Creasing: Making a 'pinch' mark in a piece of paper to alter its shape slightly. It is often used for cosmetic effect, to create expression on the face of a model of an animal, for example.

Diagrams: There are certain conventions in drawing that you should know. A line made up of dots and dashes indicates the centre line of a piece of paper, which, when opened out, will produce a mirror image. Where parts of a mirror image glue to each other, only one of their part numbers is shown.

The amount of skill required in making the models in this book varies. Some of the projects are really very simple but others are quite demanding. Start with a relatively easy one such as the mole (page 30) or the paper posy (page 78) before attacking major projects like the goblin (page 58) or wolf (page 124). Do not feel tied to using the exact materials quoted for each project – improvise.

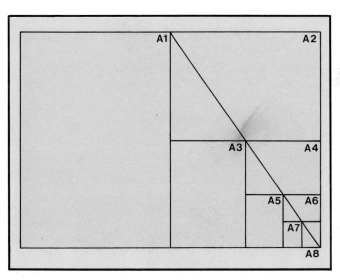

ANIMAL MAGIC

The models in this section are all straightforward designs relying on modifications of the most simple shapes (cones, tubes etc) that can be made from card.

The mole is the least demanding model, followed by, in order of difficulty, the bat, mouse, owl and dove. The dove begins to utilize 'stress' to give strength and form. The wings hold their position, not due to any thickness of paper, but because of the manner in which they are attached to the body.

Shortly after producing this design I held an exhibition in London's Covent Garden, and included two doves with the enormous wingspan of 1.52m/5ft, built from paper only twice the weight of that recommended here for a small bird.

A friend, also working in paper, felt it would never work and I must admit harbouring doubts myself. However, when the first bird was hoisted aloft the wings remained proud. This model, perhaps more than any other in the collection, demonstrates just how strong paper can be.

The simple act of folding a sheet of paper neatly in half will provide it with more potential strength and infinitely more scope than a flat

sheet. It can be balanced on its two ends like a tent, or stood on one side like an open book. In this new form it can even be used to support a lightweight object. When modelling with paper you will always get a better result with a crisp, new sheet, so experiment with folds on scrap paper first.

In the past I have adorned the owl, mouse and notoriously shortsighted mole with spectacles, a requirement which governed their size. The wearing of spectacles gives the animals an extra dimension to their characters, and it can be fun trying them with a selection of different frames.

I enjoy working with simple shapes. It feels somehow more honest to the material being used. I have often been called upon to produce really quite complex models from paper, including scientifically accurate replicas of machines. It is easy to become so wrapped up in comparative measurements and the accuracy of angles that, if anything, the paper becomes a hindrance to the sought-after effect. Obviously, this is not at all an ideal situation, but the disciplines learned by such exercises can be applied to other work and it does heighten the enjoyment of a simple, clean model.

MIGHTY MOUSE

Begin by scaling up the provided plans to the required size. The grid measurement given will build a mouse 381mm/15in in length. Any detail such as nose or eyes should be painted on the model whilst the paper is flat.

1 Cut out the head and score along the dotted lines. Apply glue to the areas shaded in the diagram and construct the head by forming the cheeks 1 to **1** then the nose 2 to **2** and 3 to **3**. Before cutting out the ears and jaw, line the brown paper with pink. This simple task very much enhances the completed model. Cut out the ears and position in slots on either side of the head. Cut out the jaw, and position it in between the cheeks.

2 Cut out the body and score along the dotted lines. To construct the body first apply glue to the areas represented by the shaded areas on the legs and assemble these parts 4 to **4**, 5 to **5**. After this, glue tabs 6 to **6** forming the curved spine of the mouse.

3 Glue tab 7 to **7** and 8 to **8**, giving the mouse its characteristic stance.

4 Cut out and crease the arm section and glue into position on the body 9 to **9**, 10 to **10** and 11 to **11**, 12 to **12**.

5 Finally glue the assembled head onto the body. You can use your own discretion as to the angle and pose of the head. The positioning of the head and jaw on this model can provide each completed mouse with a quite different expression, ranging from astonishment to mild disbelief.

6 If you wish to make a standing version of the mouse, cut out the alternative arms. Follow steps 1-3 then glue the arms into position 9 to **9**, 10 to **10** and

YOU WILL NEED:
- ☐ Scalpel or modelling knife
- ☐ Scissors
- ☐ Impact adhesive
- ☐ 1 SRA2 sheet of 200gsm brown paper
- ☐ 1 A3 sheet of 80gsm pink paper
- ☐ Black felt-tipped pen, or black paint and paintbrush
- ☐ Coathanger and string for tail

11 to **11**, 12 to **12** as on the first mouse, but on this version cut the hand pieces out of pink paper. Glue in position on completed model, 13 to **13** and 14 to **14**.
7 To make a simple but effective tail for the mouse take a metal coat hanger, untwist the hook part and bend it in such a manner as to form both a tail and also its support. Make a very small hole at the base of the mouse, poke about 50mm/2in of wire in, then bend the rest of the wire so that it curves around the mouse, looping it up to support the arms or the chest. Once the completed shape is determined, wrap and glue string around the wire to give a more realistic-looking tail effect.

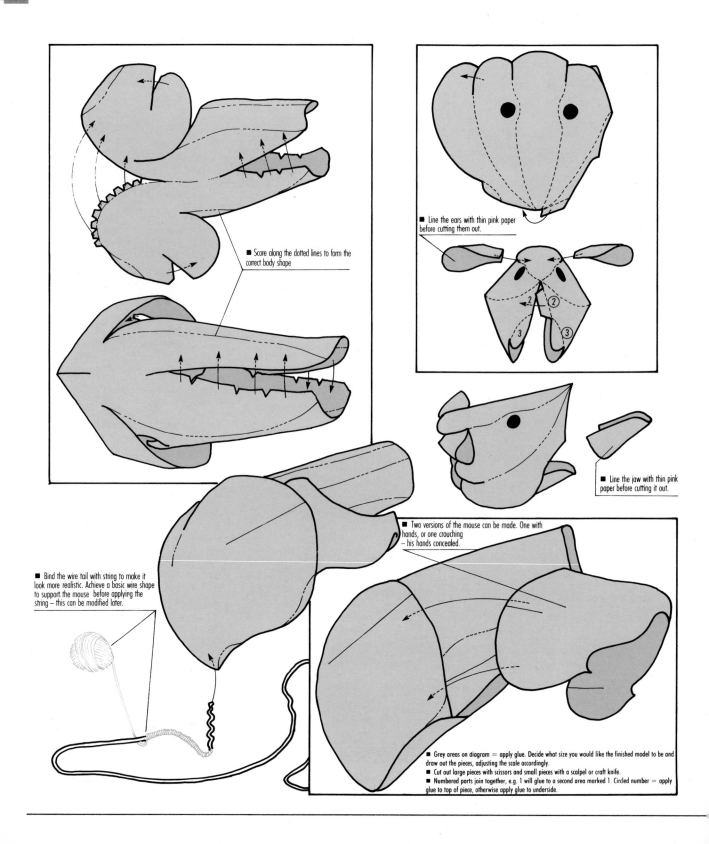

■ Score along the dotted lines to form the correct body shape

■ Line the ears with thin pink paper before cutting them out.

■ Line the jaw with thin pink paper before cutting it out.

■ Bind the wire tail with string to make it look more realistic. Achieve a basic wire shape to support the mouse before applying the string – this can be modified later.

■ Two versions of the mouse can be made. One with hands, or one crouching – his hands concealed.

■ Grey areas on diagram = apply glue. Decide what size you would like the finished model to be and draw out the pieces, adjusting the scale accordingly.
■ Cut out large pieces with scissors and small pieces with a scalpel or craft knife.
■ Numbered parts join together, e.g. 1 will glue to a second area marked 1. Circled number = apply glue to top of piece, otherwise apply glue to underside.

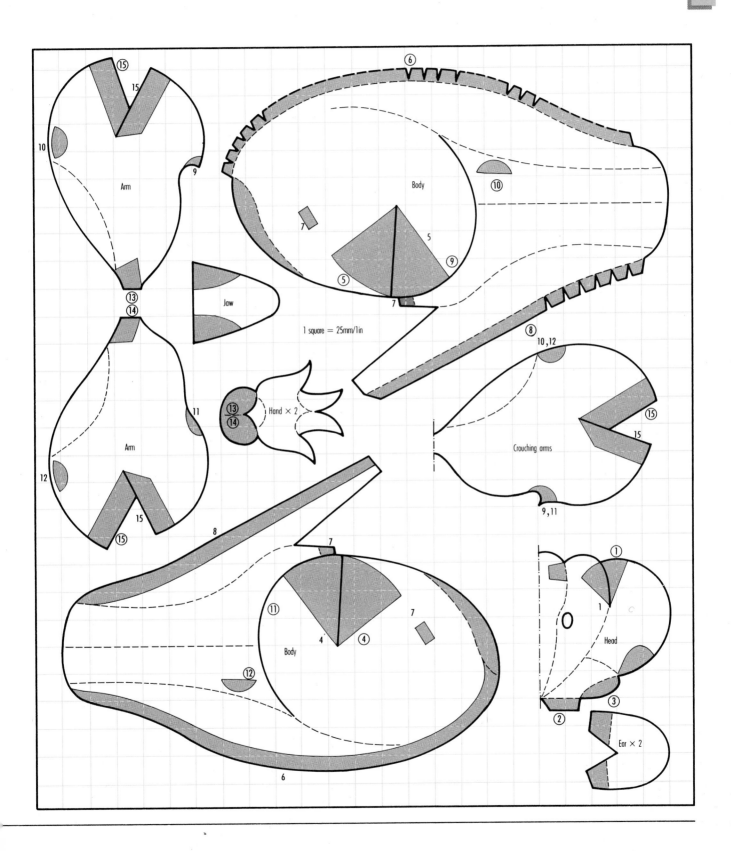

1 square = 25mm/1in

MR KNOW IT OWL

The grid measurement provided will form a completed owl 355mm/14in long.

1 Begin by cutting out the owl body from the beige paper and the underside from the 200gsm white paper. Score along dotted lines. Cut out and gently raise up the feathers on the owl's breast.

2 Glue the tabs 1 to **1** forming the breast of the owl.

3 Take the underside section and having creased it glue tabs 2 to **2**, 3 to **3** and 4 to **4**, 5 to **5**. Allow the glue to dry before completing the body by gluing 6 to **6** and 7 to **7**.

4 Before cutting out the wings, line some beige paper with the 80gsm white paper. After this has dried cut out the wings and glue into position on the body 8 to **8** and 9 to **9**.

5 Cut the head section out of beige paper. Glue tabs 10 to **10**.

6 Cut out eyes from 200gsm white paper, and the forehead from beige. Glue eyes onto forehead 13 to **13**, 14 to **14** and then glue the entire piece to the head 12 to **12**, 11 to **11**. Allow this to dry and cut out the two pieces that form the beak from the beige paper. Assemble the beak pieces by gluing tabs 15 to **15** on the upper beak and 16 to **16** on the lower.

7 Return to the head. Form the eyes by gluing 17 to **17** and 18 to **18**. Refer to the diagram and notice how the eyes appear like a cone with the summit reversed. Finally glue tabs 19 to **19**, 20 to **20** and 21 to **21**, 22 to **22**.

8 Glue the upper beak into position 23 to **23** and the lower beak 24 to **24**.

9 To provide your completed model with more stability place a coin inside the body of the owl just behind the tail. He will now perch on any surface.

YOU WILL NEED:
- Scalpel or modelling knife
- Scissors
- Impact adhesive
- 1 SRA2 sheet of 200gsm beige paper
- 1 A3 sheet of 80gsm white paper
- 1 A3 sheet of 200gsm white paper

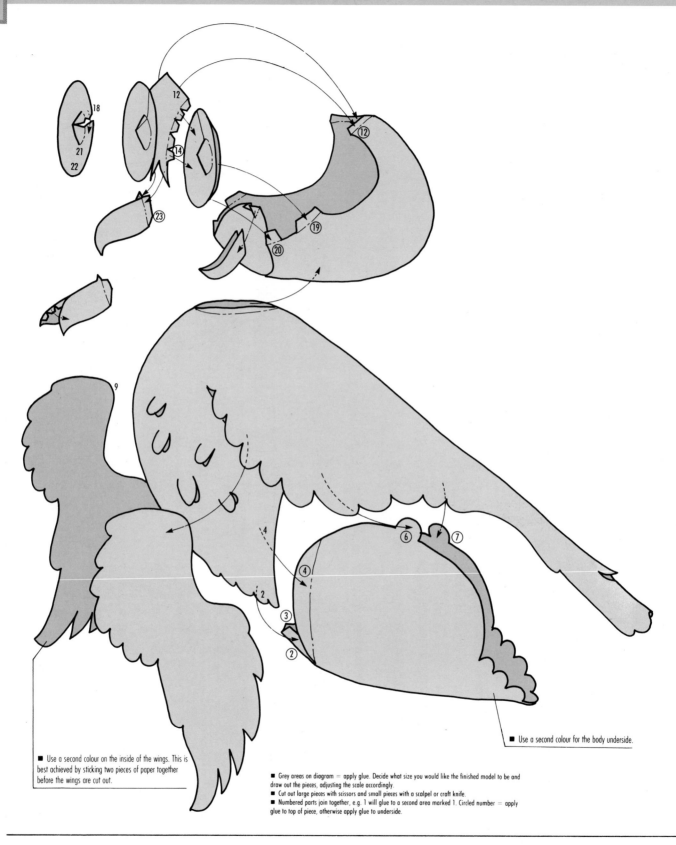

18
21
22

12
14
23

12
19
20
9

4
2
3
2
6
7
4

■ Use a second colour for the body underside.

■ Use a second colour on the inside of the wings. This is best achieved by sticking two pieces of paper together before the wings are cut out.

■ Grey areas on diagram = apply glue. Decide what size you would like the finished model to be and draw out the pieces, adjusting the scale accordingly.
■ Cut out large pieces with scissors and small pieces with a scalpel or craft knife.
■ Numbered parts join together, e.g. 1 will glue to a second area marked 1. Circled number = apply glue to top of piece, otherwise apply glue to underside.

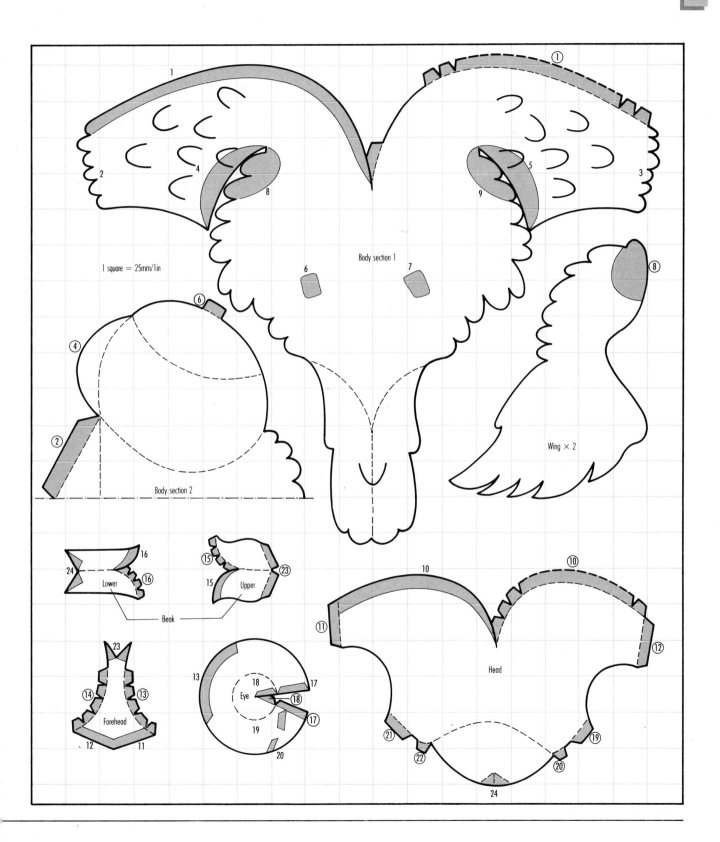

1

① ①

2

4

8

5

9

3

1 square = 25mm/1in

Body section 1

6

7

⑧ 8

⑥ 6

④ 4

Wing × 2

② 2

Body section 2

16

24 ⑯ 16

Lower

⑮ 15

15

⑳ 23

Upper

Beak

23

⑩ 10

10

⑭ 14   ⑬ 13

⑪ 11

Head

⑫ 12

Forehead

12   11

13

18

Eye

17

⑱ 18

⑰ 17

19

20

㉑ 21

㉒ 22

⑲ 19

⑳ 20

24

VAMPAPER BAT

The grid measurement provided here will make a bat with a 558mm/22in wingspan.

1 Scale up the model to the required size and paint in any detail (e.g. black eyes and nose, white fangs) before construction.

2 Cut out the head front section, glue 1 to **1**, 2 to **2** to form the nose and 3 to **3**, 4 to **4** to form the snout.

3 Before cutting the head back section, line the brown paper with pink paper to enhance the completed model. Also line the ears before cutting.

4 Cut out the head back section and glue tabs 5 to **5**.

5 Attach the head front section to the back section by gluing tabs 6 to **6** and 7 to **7**. Allow this to dry before completing the head by gluing 8 to **8**, 9 to **9** and 10 to **10**, 11 to **11**.

6 Slot the ears into position 12 to **12**; glue 13 to **13** and 14 to **14**.

7 Turn to the body section. Glue tabs 15 to **15**, 16 to **16**, then 17 to **17**, 18 to **18** and 19 to **19**, 20 to **20**. While this is drying cut out the wings.

8 Returning to the body, glue 21 to **21** and then glue the entire body on to the wing section, referring to the diagram for guidance.

9 Attach the head to the body using your own discretion for positioning.

10 Cut out two feet. These are identical to those of the mouse (see pages 16-17). Glue them to the legs.

11 Your bat can be hung upside down from virtually anything by using two short pieces of wire (unravelled paperclips for instance). Hook one end of each piece into each foot and the other onto whatever you wish the bat to hang from, say a picture rail or light fitting.

YOU WILL NEED:
- ☐ Scalpel or modelling knife
- ☐ Scissors
- ☐ Impact adhesive
- ☐ 3 SRA2 sheets of 200gsm brown paper
- ☐ 1 A3 sheet of 80gsm pink paper
- ☐ Black felt-tipped pen, or black paint and paintbrush
- ☐ White paint and paintbrush

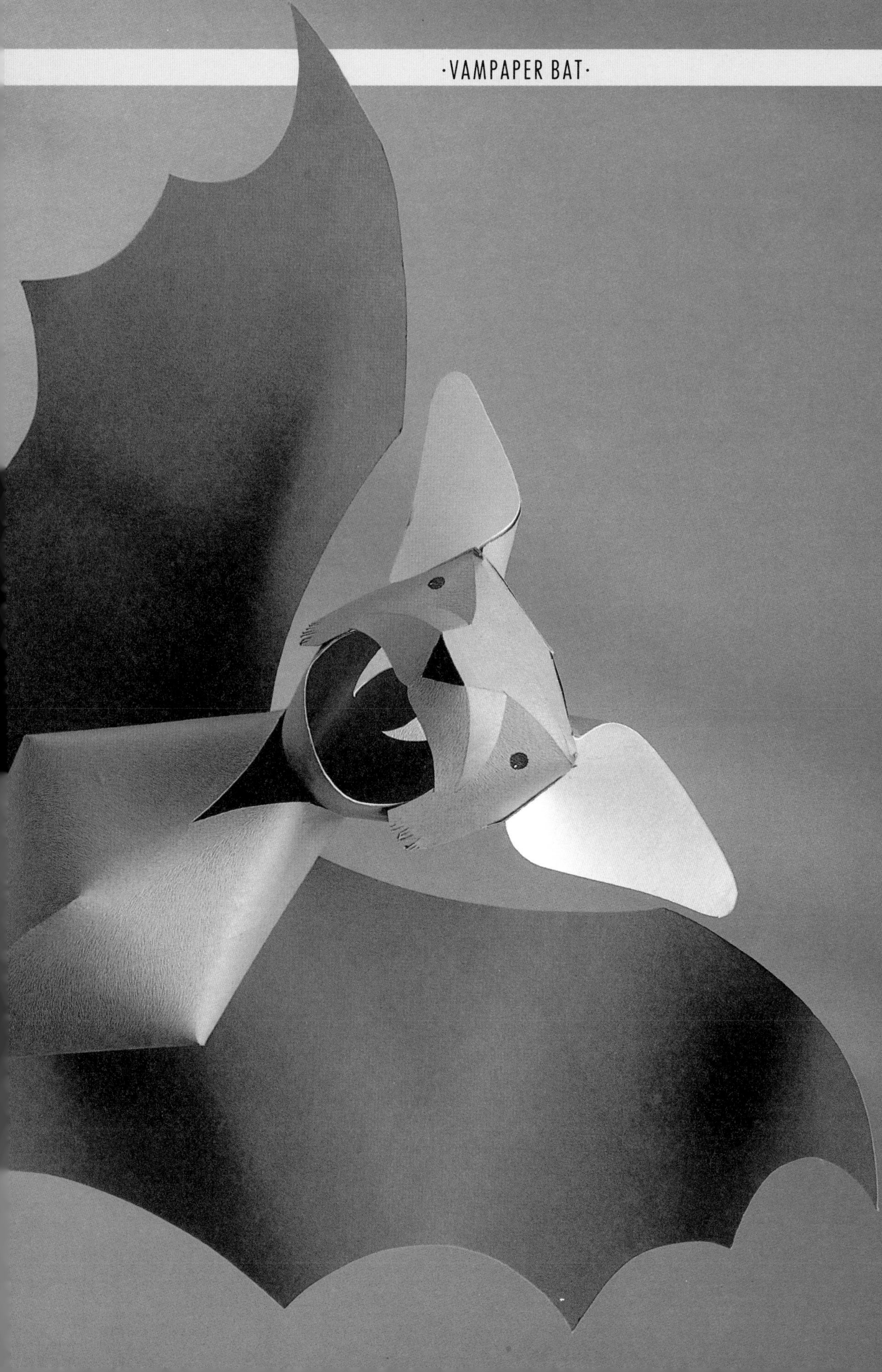

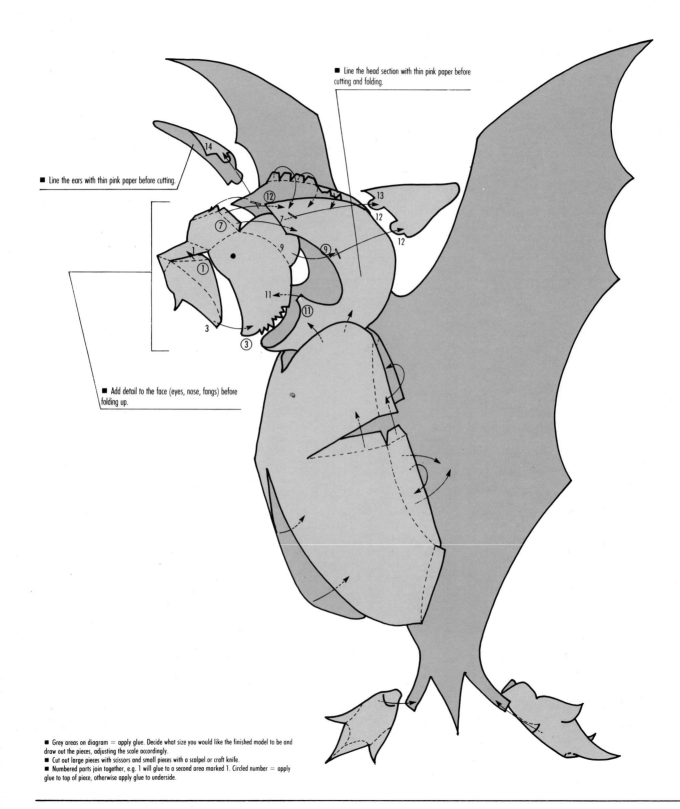

■ Line the head section with thin pink paper before cutting and folding.

■ Line the ears with thin pink paper before cutting.

■ Add detail to the face (eyes, nose, fangs) before folding up.

■ Grey areas on diagram = apply glue. Decide what size you would like the finished model to be and draw out the pieces, adjusting the scale accordingly.
■ Cut out large pieces with scissors and small pieces with a scalpel or craft knife.
■ Numbered parts join together, e.g. 1 will glue to a second area marked 1. Circled number = apply glue to top of piece, otherwise apply glue to underside.

Foot × 2

22

1 square = 25mm/1in

Ear × 2

13,14

12   12

6

14

8

10

5

Head section 2

11

9

5

13

7

19

21

21

19

20

20

18

16

17

15

Body

6

19

8

Face (head section 1)

2

10

2

17

15

4   4

18   16

20   21   21   20

BIRDS OF A FEATHER

The grid measurement provided will form a dove with a wingspan of 431mm/17in.

1 Cut out and score the body. Glue tabs 1 to **1**, 2 to **2** and then tabs 3 to **3**.

2 Before cutting out the head, paint or draw in any details such as eyes, beak etc. Cut out the head, score along the dotted lines then glue tabs 4 to **4**, 5 to **5** and 6 to **6**. Finally, gently 'pinch' the beak so that it stands out by folding along the previously scored lines.

3 Form the collar by gluing 7 to **7**.

4 Cut out the two pieces to form each wing. Score along the dotted lines and gently crease these to give

the wing increased shape. Join the two pieces by gluing 8 to **8**, ensuring that they slip into the slot. Match the glue points 9 to **9** carefully as this provides the wing with all its form and strength.

5 Repeat step 4 for the second wing.
6 Attach one wing at a time to the body, again taking care to match glue points 10 to **10** and 11 to **11** as these greatly effect the poise of the wing. If you intend making several doves, notice how subtly the wings can be varied, and no two of your doves need be the same.
7 Slip the collar onto the body 12 to **12** so that the

feathery cut-outs slightly overlap the areas of each wing attached to the body.
8 Glue the head into position 13 to **13**.
9 Cut out the tail piece, glue 14 to **14** and slip the completed dove tail into position, gluing 15 to **15**.

These models can be displayed by either looping some thin cord under each wing and suspending them from the ceiling or shelves; or by attaching the flight feathers of one wing firmly to a board and hanging the board on a wall in the same way as a picture. The illustrated doves were photographed in this manner.

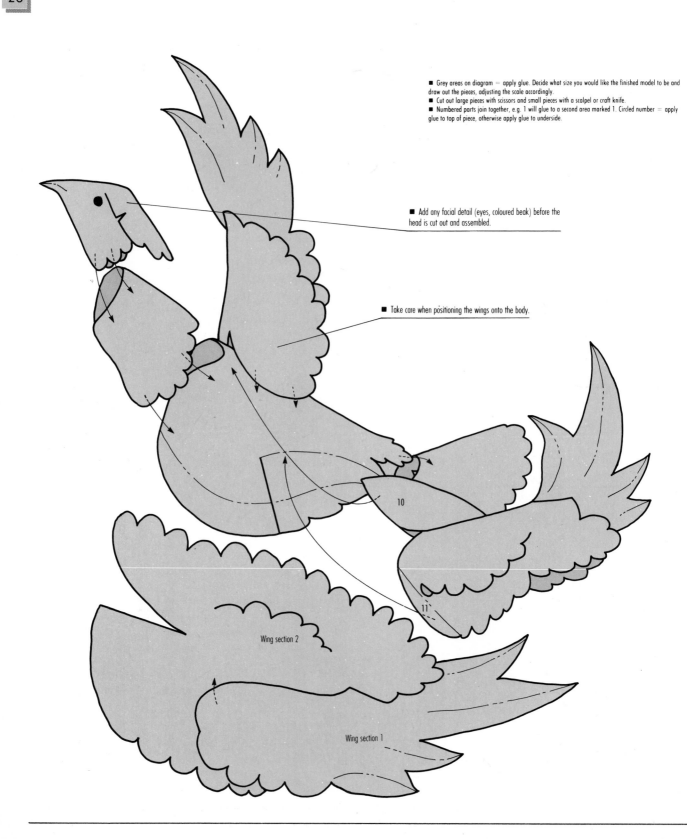

■ Grey areas on diagram = apply glue. Decide what size you would like the finished model to be and draw out the pieces, adjusting the scale accordingly.
■ Cut out large pieces with scissors and small pieces with a scalpel or craft knife.
■ Numbered parts join together, e.g. 1 will glue to a second area marked 1. Circled number = apply glue to top of piece, otherwise apply glue to underside.

■ Add any facial detail (eyes, coloured beak) before the head is cut out and assembled.

■ Take care when positioning the wings onto the body.

10

11

Wing section 2

Wing section 1

Tail

15

14

14

Wing section 1
× 2

8

9

1 square = 25mm/1in

Wing section 2
× 2

9

8

10

11

12

12

12

Collar

7

13

7

Body

1

1

11

11

10

10

12

12

12

1

2

2

3

3

15

Head

13

5

4

5

4

6

6

MOLE IN A HOLE

The grid measurement provided makes a mole 228mm/9in long.

1 Cut out the body section. Score and fold along the dotted lines and cut slots 1 and 2 before gluing 3 to **3**.

2 Cut out a foot. Before folding, paint each claw white (this may take more than one coat). When the paint is dry glue 4 to **4** and glue each claw together 6 to **6**, 7 to **7**, 8 to **8**, and 9 to **9**.

3 Attach the foot to the body by placing tab 1 into slot 1. Gluing the tab in is not compulsory. It depends whether you would like the mole's feet to be moveable or not.

4 Repeat sections steps 2 and 3 for the second foot.

5 Cut out the head, Before assembly add any fine detail such as the eyes and nose.

6 Form the cheek by gluing 10 to **10** on each side of the head. Glue 11 to **11** and 12 to **12** to make the nose.

7 Before cutting out the jaw, line the brown paper with a piece of pink paper. This will enhance the completed model. Cut out the jaw and curl it gently around a pencil to give it shape. Glue it into position between the cheeks 13 to **13**, 14 to **14**. The expression of the mole can be altered quite

YOU WILL NEED:
- ☐ Scalpel or modelling knife
- ☐ Scissors
- ☐ Impact adhesive
- ☐ 1 SRA2 sheet of 200gsm dark brown paper
- ☐ 1 A3 sheet of 80gsm pink paper
- ☐ A black felt-tipped pen
- ☐ White paint and paintbrush

dramatically by varying the positioning of the jaw, so that part I will leave up to you.

As you will have noticed, the mole is designed to look as if he has just emerged from a hole, so he can be displayed appearing from a desk top, the floor or any other flat surface. Enhance this effect by placing a little wreckage around him, to represent the discarded rubble from his hole.

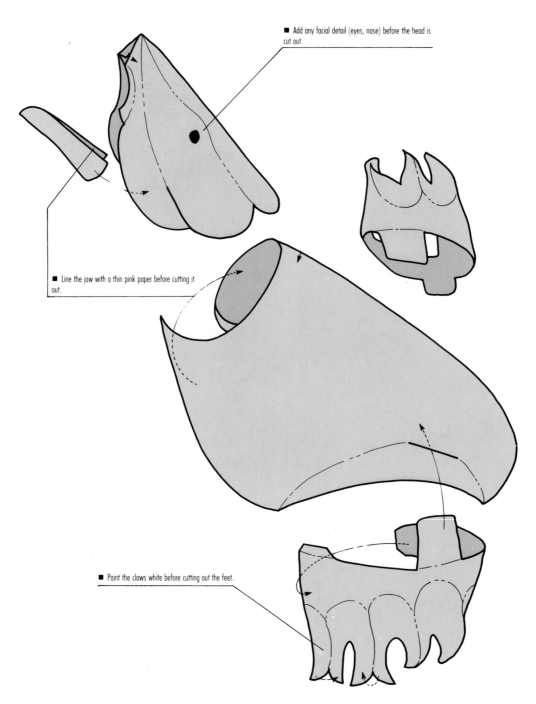

■ Add any facial detail (eyes, nose) before the head is cut out.

■ Line the jaw with a thin pink paper before cutting it out.

■ Paint the claws white before cutting out the feet.

■ Grey areas on diagram = apply glue. Decide what size you would like the finished model to be and draw out the pieces, adjusting the scale accordingly.
■ Cut out large pieces with scissors and small pieces with a scalpel or craft knife.
■ Numbered parts join together, e.g. 1 will glue to a second area marked 1. Circled number = apply glue to top of piece, otherwise apply glue to underside.

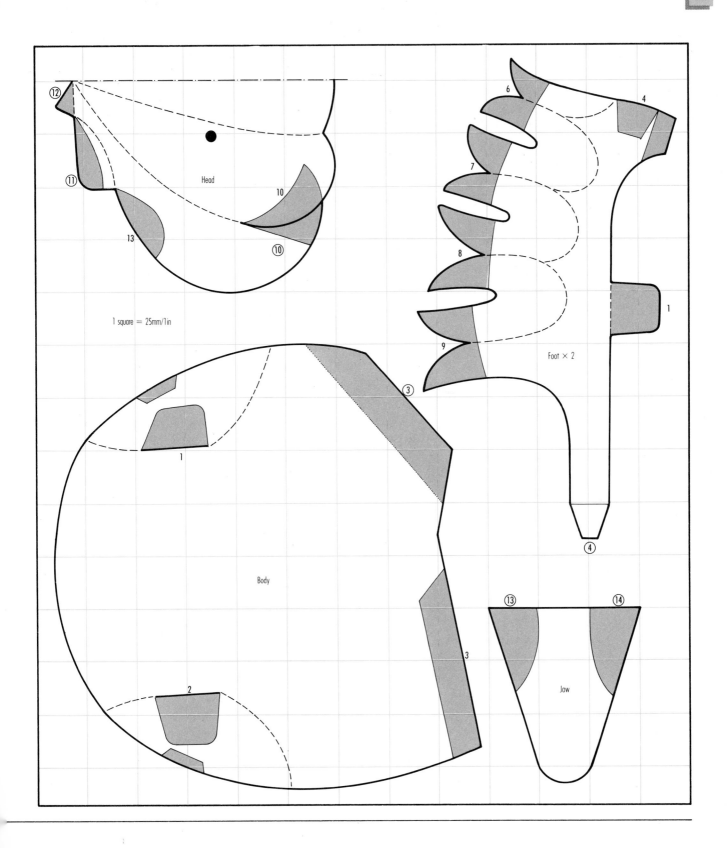

12

11

Head

13

10

10

1 square = 25mm/1in

6

4

7

8

9

1

Foot × 2

3

1

Body

4

2

3

13

14

Jaw

PASTE JEWELLERY

This chapter on jewellery-making is easily the most straightforward section in the book, but it does rely on careful and competent cutting. All the ideas centre on the use of visually interesting papers rather than on any elaborate folding or construction techniques. Of course, the choice of paper you use for these projects is entirely personal, although gold and silver metallic-effect papers seem to suggest themselves for jewellery, not least because they will reflect the light when worn.

Working on such small pieces of paper it is virtually impossible to attempt anything but the most simple forms without it becoming too fiddly, and the project getting covered with ridiculous amounts of glue. To spare everyone such problems these are easy projects that use colour and decoration to create effect, although a

number of different styles have been used. Both the 'gilty party' necklace, with its skeletal autumn leaves, and the butterfly hair comb employ the use of filigree cutting techniques. The result is very intricate-looking, quite unlike the modern, cubist shapes of the earrings and the crisp, clean lines of the bracelet. Beginners should start with the earrings or the simple, interwoven loops of the lover's knot brooch.

The ideas are, to some extent, interchangeable. For instance, make two scaled-down lover's knot brooches, attach them to earclips and you have a pair of earrings; the necklace can be shortened to make a bracelet just as a longer verson of the bracelet could be worn, choker-fashion around the neck. Mount the butterfly on a pin for an alternative to the brooch, or do the same with one of the cubist earrings.

CUBIST CLIPS

YOU WILL NEED:
- ☐ Scalpel or modelling knife
- ☐ Impact adhesive
- ☐ 2 small squares (approximately 50 × 50mm/2 × 2in) of contrasting but complementary coloured paper (for example, 1 matt and 1 metallic), for each earring
- ☐ 1 pair of ear clips
- ☐ Fine, strong twine

1   Line the two squares of different coloured paper by sticking one on top of the other.
2   Cut along the lines with a scalpel, and score along the dotted lines.
3   Fold the scored lines marked A forward. Fold the scored lines marked B backwards.
4   Repeat steps 1 to 3 for the second earring.
5   Using a small length of twine attach the rings to the ear clips.

   The novelty of this design relies on the way the two contrasting colours play against each other, and the three-dimensional effect of the folds. Literally thousands of variations on this idea can be created. Simple cuts and folds that allow you to see one side of the paper through the other can be very effective and are easy to make. This idea could easily be extended for matching necklace and bracelet projects.

LOVER'S KNOT

YOU WILL NEED:
- ☐ Scalpel, or modelling knife or scissors
- ☐ Impact adhesive
- ☐ 2 strips (approximately 101 × 12mm/4 × ½in) of mauve and silver paper
- ☐ 1 pencil (to create curves)
- ☐ 1 brooch mount pin

This is a very simple project, and you will probably be able to complete it just by referring to the photograph and diagram.

1 Take the mauve and silver papers and glue them together, back to back.

2 Cut out the two sections. Curl the areas marked with dotted lines around a pencil to provide a smooth curve.

3 Glue 1 to **1**.

4 Consulting the diagram, thread the second section into the first and glue 2 to **2**.

Once again, this item relies for its appeal upon the contrast between the two papers. As the two sections entwine with each other you will see both colours. Paper can be threaded in almost as many ways as ribbon, so again the possibilities are limitless.

CUBIST CLIPS

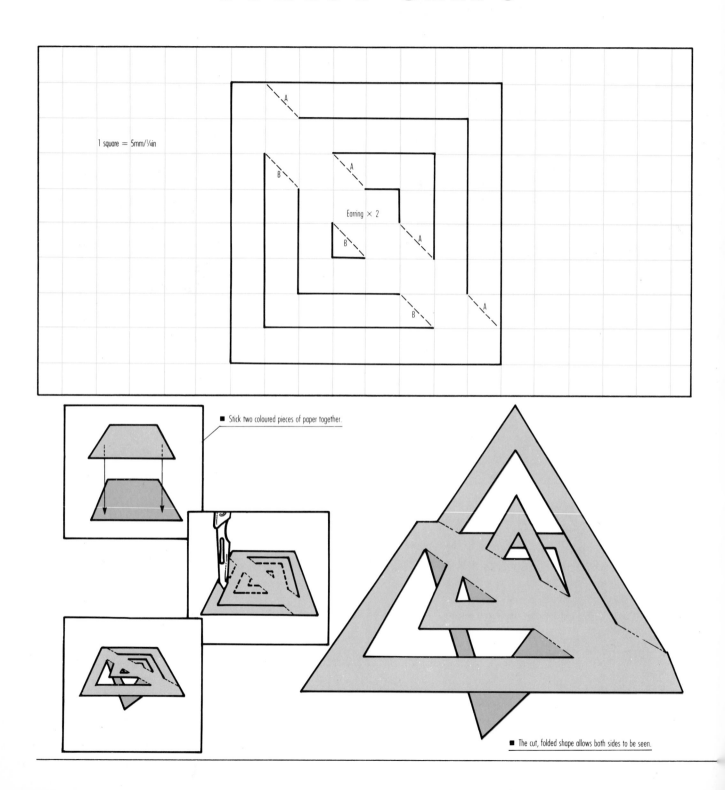

1 square = 5mm/¼in

A

A

B

Earring × 2

B

A

A

B

■ Stick two coloured pieces of paper together.

■ The cut, folded shape allows both sides to be seen.

LOVER'S KNOT

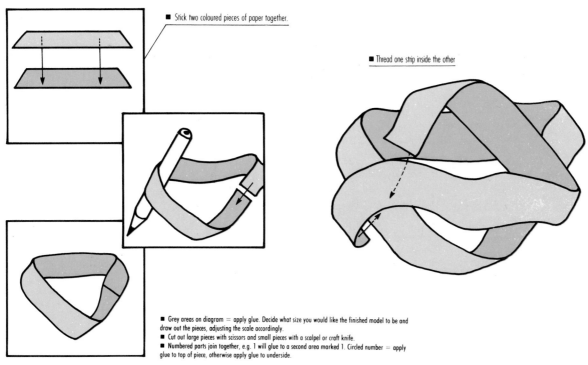

■ Stick two coloured pieces of paper together.

■ Thread one strip inside the other

■ Grey areas on diagram = apply glue. Decide what size you would like the finished model to be and draw out the pieces, adjusting the scale accordingly.
■ Cut out large pieces with scissors and small pieces with a scalpel or craft knife.
■ Numbered parts join together, e.g. 1 will glue to a second area marked 1. Circled number = apply glue to top of piece, otherwise apply glue to underside.

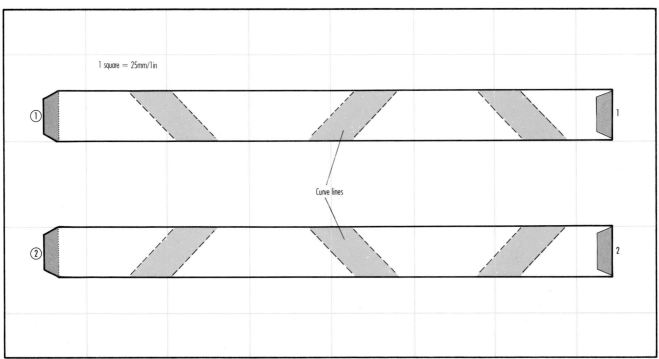

1 square = 25mm/1in

Curve lines

BUTTERFLY COMB

As with all the projects in this section, this piece relies on delicate cutting and choice of attractive papers for success. All elaborate constructions have been abandoned temporarily.

1 Carefully cut out the filigree pattern from the black paper or the bright metallic paper. Choose a colour that will stand out, either for its contrast with the base wing paper or for its glittery quality. Many metallic papers will need to be mounted upon a piece of card to give them added thickness.

2 Cut out the base wing from a coloured paper. This can be plain. Decoration can be added with tissues, metallic papers, doilies etc, to give a light, feathery appearance.

3 Glue the filigree-patterned wing on to the decorated base wing, 1 to **1**. Apply glue only to the underside of the body and the filigree wing, ensuring that the wing can be lifted away from the base wing.

4 Attach the underside of the body to a hair slide or hair comb using strong glue.

The butterfly can be made in two different ways. A profile butterfly is made by cutting just one filigree wing and one base wing. An alternative idea is to cut two filigree-patterned wings and two base wings, making an open-winged butterfly as though viewed from above. Fantastically contrasting butterflies can be made by selecting varied and imaginative papers. Do not hesitate to utilize wallpaper, wrapping paper and tin foil to create decoration. I have made this one into a hair comb, but a smaller version could easily become a brooch, or made in pairs, earrings.

YOU WILL NEED:
- Scalpel or modelling knife
- Impact adhesive
- 1 A4 sheet of 200gsm black or metallic paper
- 1 A4 sheet of 200gsm coloured paper
- Various tissue papers and doilies for additional decoration
- Hair slide or comb on which to mount completed butterfly

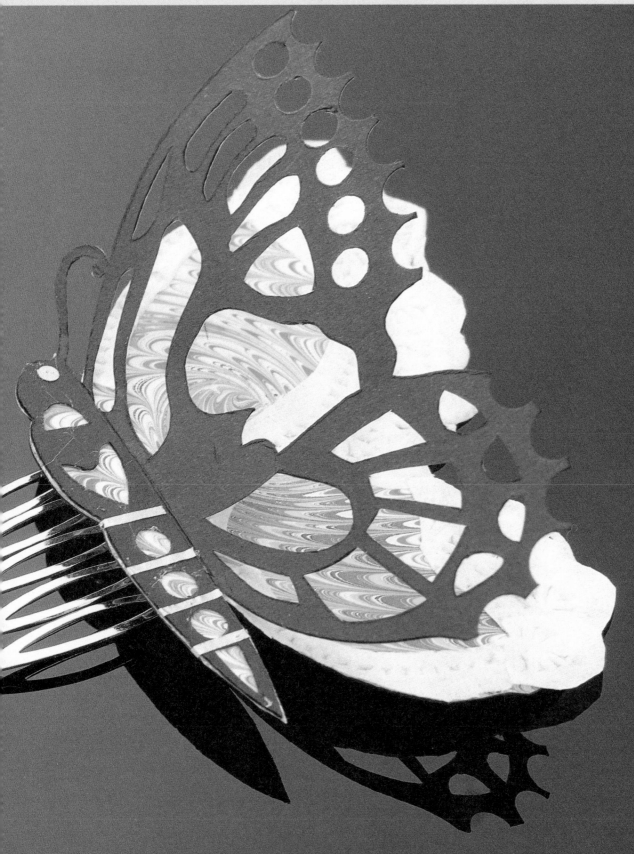

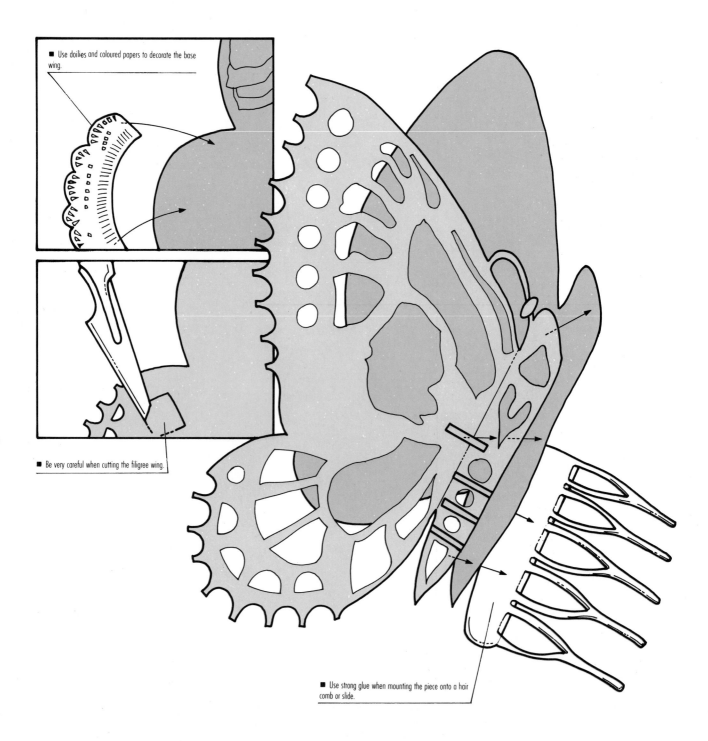

■ Use doilies and coloured papers to decorate the base wing.

■ Be very careful when cutting the filigree wing.

■ Use strong glue when mounting the piece onto a hair comb or slide.

■ Grey areas on diagram = apply glue. Decide what size you would like the finished model to be and draw out the pieces, adjusting the scale accordingly.
■ Cut out large pieces with scissors and small pieces with a scalpel or craft knife.
■ Numbered parts join together, e.g. 1 will glue to a second area marked 1. Circled number = apply glue to top of piece, otherwise apply glue to underside.

1 square = 5mm/¼in

Filigree wing

1

Base wing

①

GILTY PARTY

YOU WILL NEED:
- ☐ Scalpel or modelling knife
- ☐ Impact adhesive
- ☐ 1 A3 sheet of 200gsm silver or gold paper
- ☐ 1 A3 sheet of 200gsm coloured paper
- ☐ Tissues and decorative materials
- ☐ Drinking straws
- ☐ Fine, strong twine
- ☐ A fastener

The method of assembly for each leaf is identical even if the leaves vary in shape or size.

1 Cut out a base leaf from plain paper. This can be decorated with overlapping layers of coloured tissue, doilies or tiny pieces of household silver foil.

2 With much care, cut out the filigree leaf from a metallic silver or gold paper.

3 Apply tiny blobs of glue and attach only the stem and each leaf point to the base leaf. You will discover that the filigree leaf is, in fact, a little larger than the base leaf, and by tacking each point you will cause the filigree leaf to bow away from the base one. This is desirable, and you should not attempt to stick the delicate filigree leaf down firmly.

4 Apply a small spot of glue to the top and bottom sections of the stem, leaving the middle section free for the twine to be threaded through.

5 Repeat steps 1 to 4 with the other leaves. Cover several drinking straws with gold adhesive tape, then cut them up into 5mm/¼in lengths. Thread the completed leaves on to a fine, strong twine, spacing each with a decorated length of drinking straw.

As with the butterfly comb, considerable variation in leaves can be achieved by selecting different forms of decoration for the base leaves. Naturally the filigree leaf in each case should be cut from a metallic paper that matches the decoration applied to the base.

As paper catches for jewellery can be a little delicate and difficult to join and open behind the head I recommend the use of a metal catch bought from a craft shop, which can be stuck to the paper.

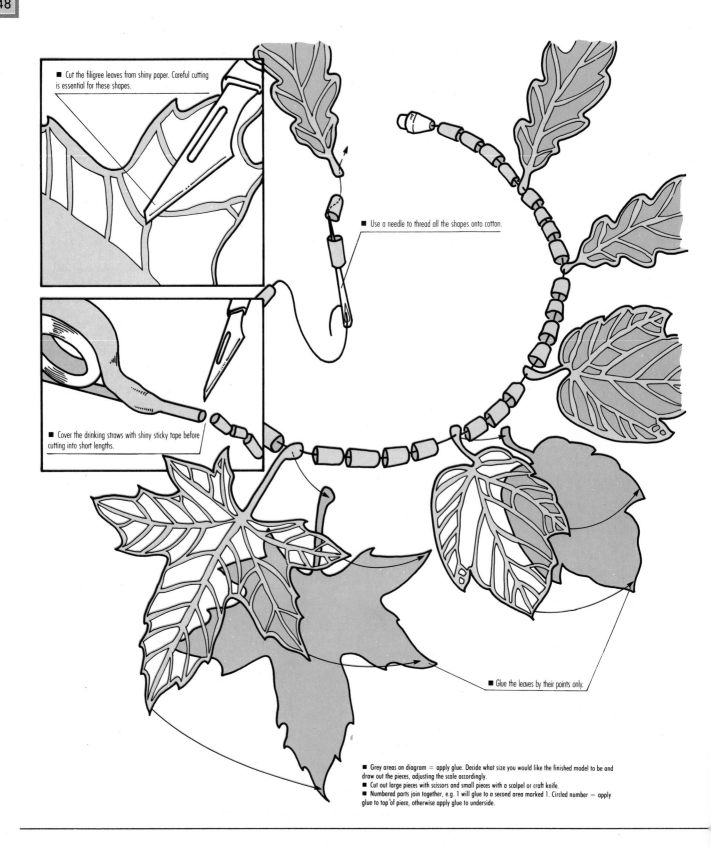

■ Cut the filigree leaves from shiny paper. Careful cutting is essential for these shapes.

■ Use a needle to thread all the shapes onto cotton.

■ Cover the drinking straws with shiny sticky tape before cutting into short lengths.

■ Glue the leaves by their points only.

■ Grey areas on diagram = apply glue. Decide what size you would like the finished model to be and draw out the pieces, adjusting the scale accordingly.
■ Cut out large pieces with scissors and small pieces with a scalpel or craft knife.
■ Numbered parts join together, e.g. 1 will glue to a second area marked 1. Circled number = apply glue to top of piece, otherwise apply glue to underside.

1 square = 5mm/¼in

Filigree leaves
× 4

Base leaves
× 4

ACES HIGH

1 Cut out the bracelet band. Carefully score along the dotted lines and cut along the solid lines. Fold along the dotted lines. When folding the slashed sections push alternate sections in, and pull the remainder out. Consult the diagram for guidance.

2 Place squares of paper from your second chosen colour onto the solid, uncut areas of the band 1 to **1**, 2 to **2**, 3 to **3**, and 4 to **4**.

3 Before any cutting or scoring is undertaken on the decorations, line these pieces with your second coloured paper. When this is completed cut along the solid lines and fold out the shapes (in this instance playing card symbols have been used, but you can use any symmetrical image) and glue 5 to **5**, 6 to **6**, 7 to 7, 8 to **8**.

4 Attach each decoration to the solid, uncut areas on the band, 9 to **9**, 10 to **10**, 11 to **11**, 12 to **12**, 13 to **13**, 14 to **14**, 15 to **15** and 16 to **16**.

5 Use a bracelet catch you have bought from a craft or hobby shop to secure the completed piece. A metallic catch will last longer than a paper fastener.

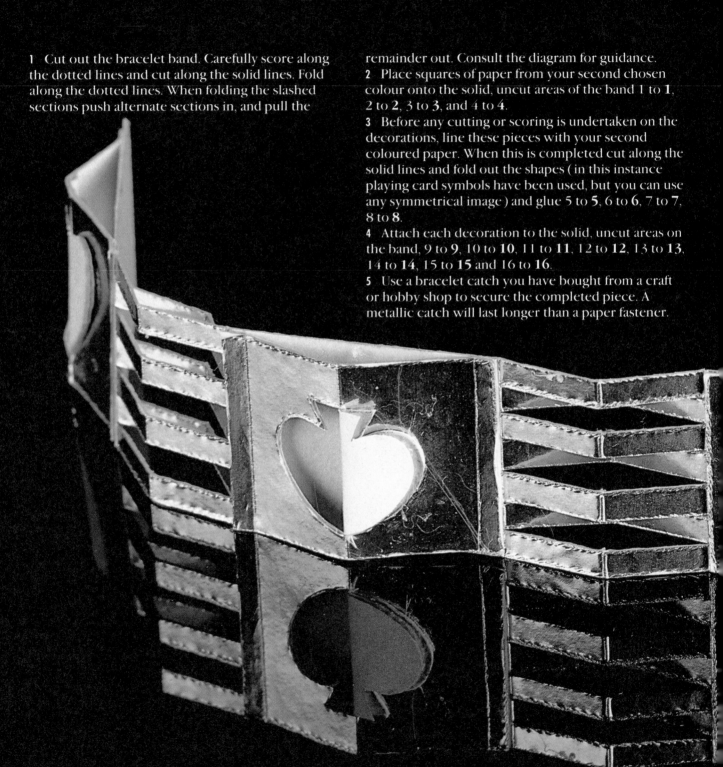

YOU WILL NEED:
- Scalpel or modelling knife
- Impact adhesive
- 1 A4 sheet of 200gsm gold paper
- 1 A4 sheet of 80gsm pink or blue paper
- 1 bracelet catch

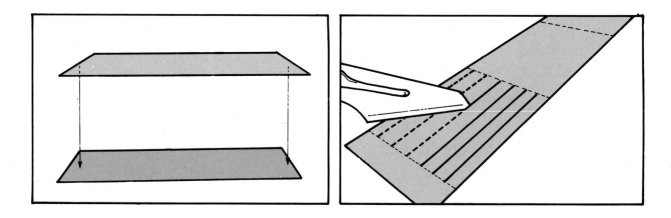

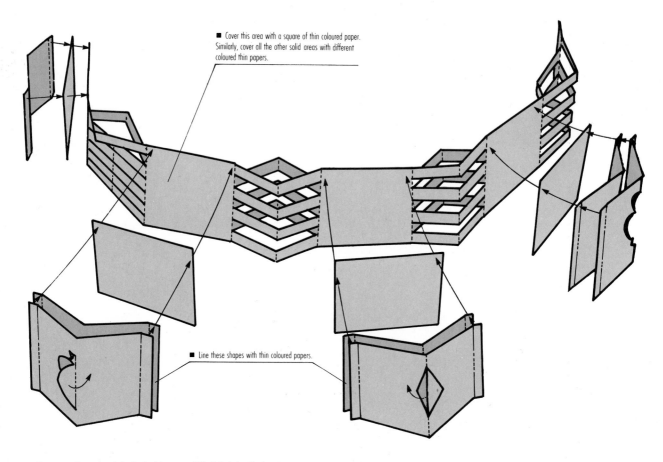

■ Cover this area with a square of thin coloured paper. Similarly, cover all the other solid areas with different coloured thin papers.

■ Line these shapes with thin coloured papers.

■ Grey areas on diagram = apply glue. Decide what size you would like the finished model to be and draw out the pieces, adjusting the scale accordingly.
■ Cut out large pieces with scissors and small pieces with a scalpel or craft knife.
■ Numbered parts join together, e.g. 1 will glue to a second area marked 1. Circled number = apply glue to top of piece, otherwise apply glue to underside.

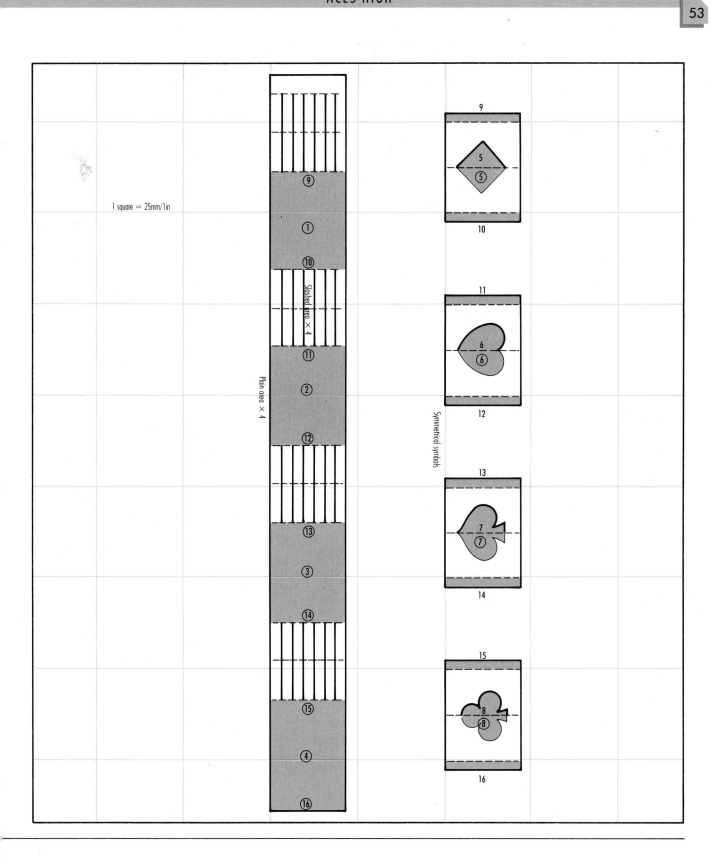

1 square = 25mm/1in

Slashed area × 4

Plain area × 4

Symmetrical symbols

·CHAPTER THREE·

TABLE TALK

I regarded this section as a real challenge. What can you produce of interest for the centre of a dinner table? Some serious thinking was needed. It is virtually impossible to find any manufactured object to place in the middle of a table which is much fun, although crackers (or snappers) always create a lot of enjoyment at Christmas. I wondered if a table centre which held gifts, or indeed was a gift in itself, would work. This became the theme for the section.

Each table centre is designed for a particular occasion — apart from the paper flowers, which can be used at any time, or in any place. I considered each of the special times of year when people might decide to throw a thematic dinner party, such as Hallowe'en, Christmas, New Year's Eve or birthdays, but of course, you can have a dinner party on any occasion; it just requires a little imagination and enterprise to make it unique, and send the guests home full of admiration at your creativity.

The gifts you present in each case I leave to your discretion, but thinking you may find the ideal Hallowe'en gift a little tricky (I mean, who wants to be given a slug, toad, or a pair of newt eyes on any occasion let alone in the middle of dinner) I recommend charms from the rowan tree (Mountain Ash) and other trees to protect your guests from the evil, mischievous spirits that are undoubtedly abroad at this time of year (more information on this in the Goblin Guest section).

You may find the idea of making a table centre, plus all the hard work of cooking and serving a meal for several people rather daunting, but if you start on your paper sculpture well in advance there should be no problems. The beauty of a table centre made from paper is that, after the meal is over, it can be dusted down and put away to await the next occasion. Plus the fact that a huge paper model in the middle of a dinner table is bound to give even the most bashful guest something to talk about to his/her neighbour. You may even find people will come to see the table centre forgetting about the meal altogether.

After working on this section I came to the conclusion that table centres can be really very interesting — so interesting in fact, that it seems a pity to wait for a dinner party to try one.

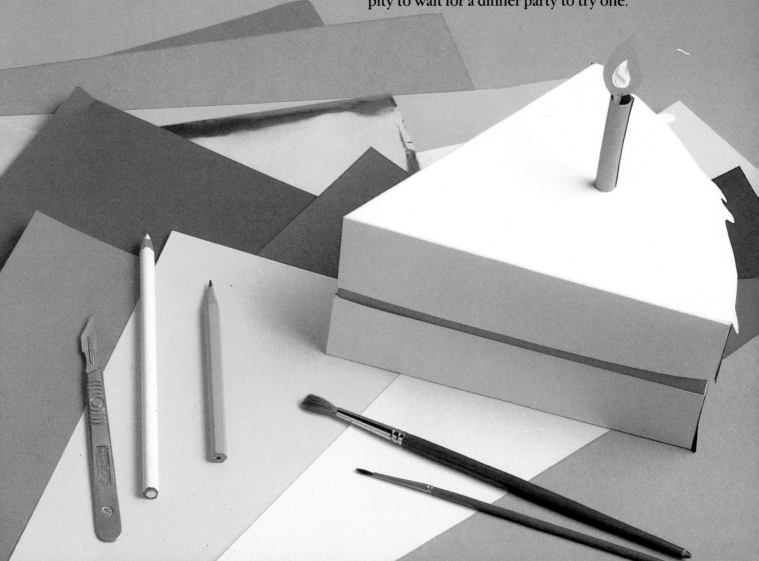

GOBLIN GUEST

YOU WILL NEED:
- ☐ Scalpel or modelling knife
- ☐ Scissors
- ☐ Impact adhesive
- ☐ 1 A2 sheet of 200gsm flesh-coloured paper
- ☐ 1 A2 sheet of 200gsm brown paper
- ☐ 1 A2 sheet of 250gsm fawn paper
- ☐ 1 A2 sheet of 250gsm green paper
- ☐ 1 A3 sheet of 200gsm red paper
- ☐ Scraps of coloured paper for hair and other details
- ☐ White and green paint
- ☐ Rowan twigs and berries

The grid measurement provided will build a goblin 457mm/18in tall.

1 Cut out the head section. Only half the section is given here but you simply draw a mirror image on the centre line. Score along the dotted lines.

2 Cut out the ears and slip into place while gluing 1 to **1** on the head section. Glue tabs 2 to **2**, 4 to **4**.

3 Form the cheeks by gluing 5 to **5** and 6 to **6**.

4 Cut out two eyes. Score along the dotted lines and, using the diagram and illustration for guidance, fold into shape and glue 7 to **7**. If you have previously tackled any of the monsters, this will be simple. Glue the eyes into position on the head section 8 to **8** and 9 to **9**.

5 Cut out the nose. Fold along the dotted lines just to loosen them. Glue 10 to **10** and 11 to **11**. Use the diagram for reference while assembling the nose. Carefully glue tab 12 to **12** inside the nose to form the nostrils.

6 Attach the nose to the head by gluing 13 to **13**, and glue 14 to **14**.

7 Cut out the upper and lower jaws. Take care while trimming the teeth, then paint them white.

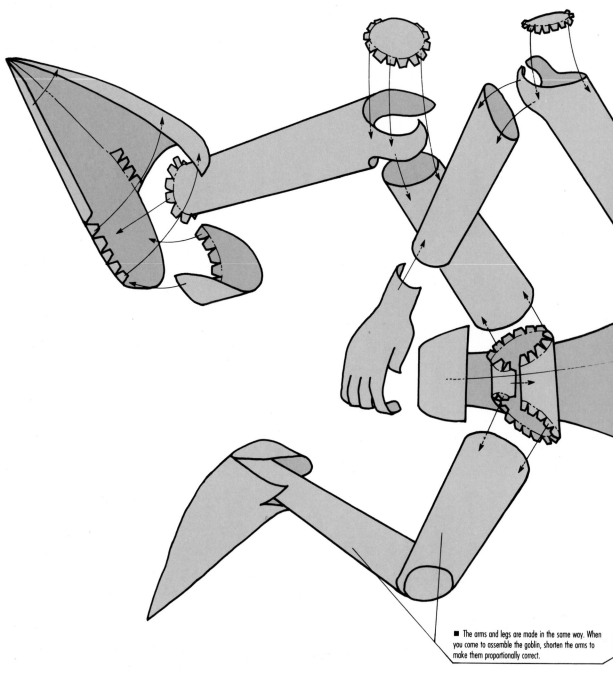

■ The arms and legs are made in the same way. When you come to assemble the goblin, shorten the arms to make them proportionally correct.

■ Grey areas on diagram = apply glue. Decide what size you would like the finished model to be and draw out the pieces, adjusting the scale accordingly.
■ Cut out large pieces with scissors and small pieces with a scalpel or craft knife.
■ Numbered parts join together, e.g. 1 will glue to a second area marked 1. Circled number = apply glue to top of piece, otherwise apply glue to underside.

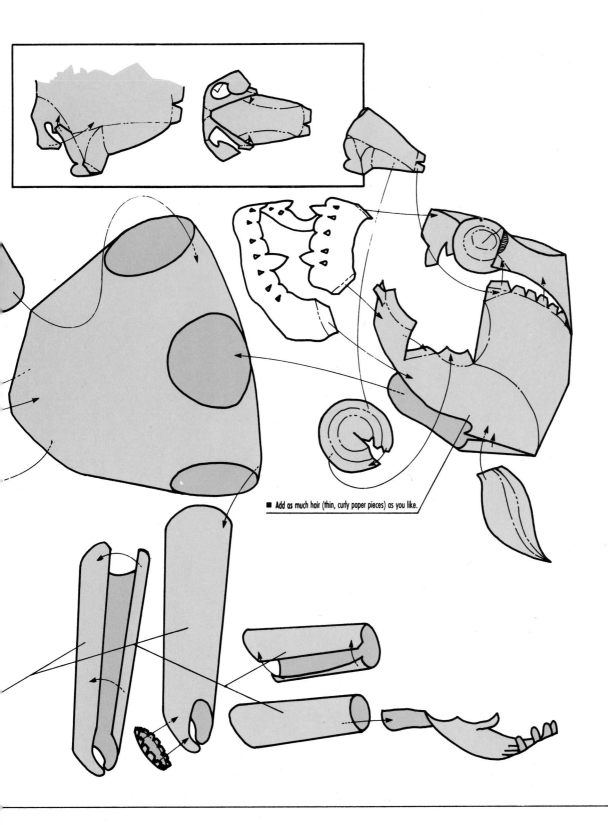

■ Add as much hair (thin, curly paper pieces) as you like.

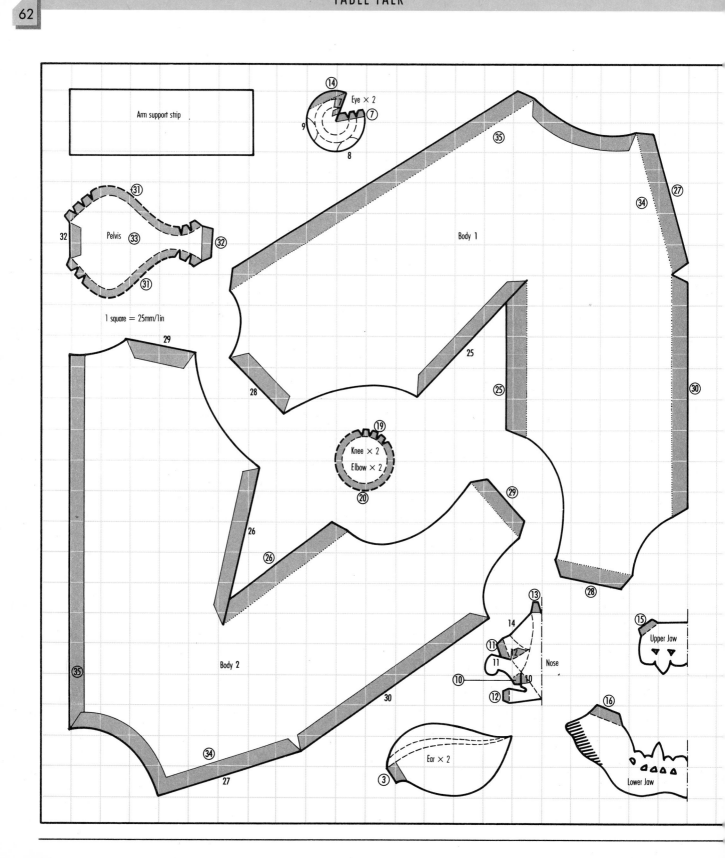

Arm support strip

Eye × 2

Pelvis

1 square = 25mm/1in

Body 1

Body 2

Knee × 2
Elbow × 2

Nose

Upper Jaw

Ear × 2

Lower Jaw

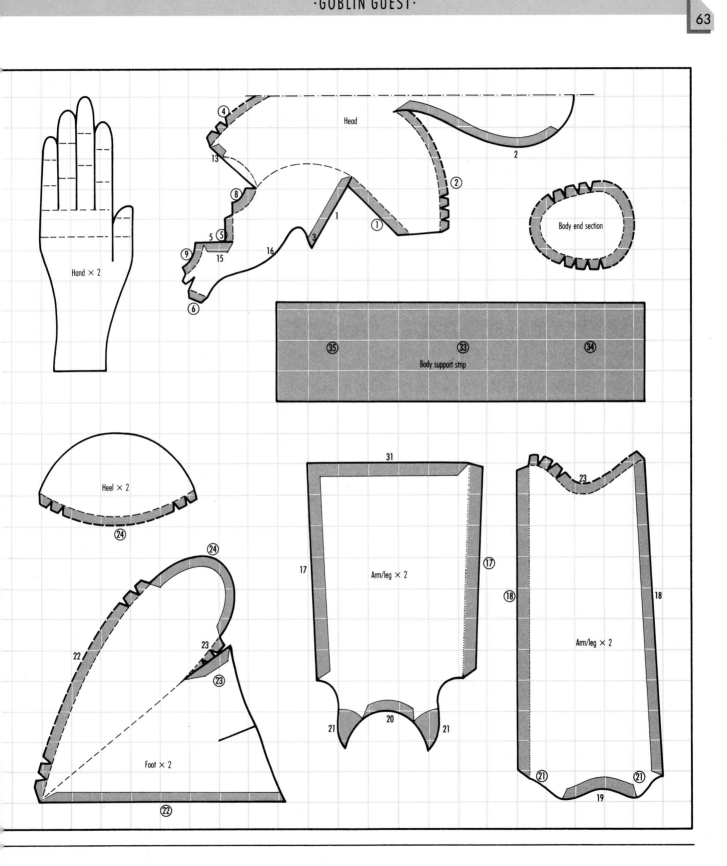

Hand × 2

Head

2

2

1

3

16

15

5 5

8

13

4

9

6

Body end section

35 33 34

Body support strip

Heel × 2

24

24

22

23

23

23

Foot × 2

22

31

Arm/leg × 2

17 17

21 20 21

23

18 18

Arm/leg × 2

21 21

19

8 Stick the upper jaw into position on the head 15 to **15**, and then the lower jaw 16 to **16**.

9 Cut strips of hair to enhance the appearance of the head, and curl them randomly to give a straggly effect.

10 The leg and arm sections are identical. The arms will need to be shortened to make them proportionally correct but this is best achieved later when you are attaching all the limbs to the body.

11 Cut out an upper leg, lower leg and knee cap. Gently roll the upper leg into a tube and glue 17 to **17**. Working in the same way roll the lower legs and glue 18 to **18**. Glue tabs 19 on the knee cap onto the lower leg, then take the upper leg and glue 20 to **20**. Curve tabs 21 around the knee on the lower leg and glue firmly.

12 Cut out the feet. Glue tabs 22 to **22** to form the body of the foot. Take the leg, with the knee facing forward, and glue into position by matching tabs 23. The heel can then be added to the foot by gluing 24 to **24**.

13 Repeat steps 11 and 12 for the second leg.

14 Make up the arms as for the legs, step 11. Do not continue with the hands until the arms are in position on the body and suitably trimmed to size. The tabs used to join the feet to the legs are unnecessary on the arms, so save effort here and do not bother cutting them.

15 Cut out the body section. Glue 25 to **25** and 26 to **26**. Curve the body into a rough tube shape and glue 27 to **27** and 30 to **30**. To form the shoulders glue 28 to **28** and 29 to **29**. Finally cut out and glue the body end section into position. The tabs can be glued to the outside of the body, as ultimately they will be concealed.

16 Cut out the pelvic area. Curve it into a tube and seal it by gluing 32 to **32**.

17 This piece is to be used to join the right and left legs. Slip tabs 31 inside the upper leg on one completed limb, glue and allow to become firm

before continuing. The tabs at the opposite end of the pelvis slip into the second limb. As it is virtually impossible to exert any pressure on this join, a large amount of glue should be applied both onto the pelvis tabs and the inside of the limb to be joined. When the join is accomplished allow at least ten minutes to pass before proceeding to the next instruction.

18 Ensure that the joined legs have become firm before attempting this next stage. Cut out the body support strip. Wrap around the back of the pelvis and glue using a liberal amount of adhesive. Take the

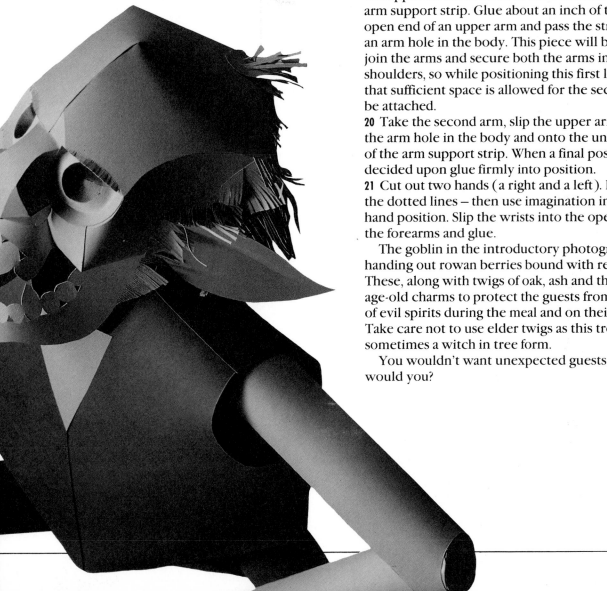

completed body and decide on the desired pose of the goblin; I suggest that the body should be angled at around 30 degrees to the ground; any angle will do but try to avoid making a goblin that topples over forwards. When a suitable angle has been decided upon glue the body support strip 35 to **35** to support the back, and 34 to **34** to hold the front. Make a good tight bond here, and provide a bit of manual support while the glue becomes firm.

19 Take the two arms and play around for a while choosing the desired stance for the goblin. Is he to be gesturing, or offering berries to someone at the table? Make the decision, then trim any excess length from the upper and lower halves of both arms. Cut out the arm support strip. Glue about an inch of this into the open end of an upper arm and pass the strip through an arm hole in the body. This piece will be used to join the arms and secure both the arms inside the shoulders, so while positioning this first limb ensure that sufficient space is allowed for the second arm to be attached.

20 Take the second arm, slip the upper arm in through the arm hole in the body and onto the unattached end of the arm support strip. When a final position is decided upon glue firmly into position.

21 Cut out two hands (a right and a left). Fold along the dotted lines – then use imagination in achieving a hand position. Slip the wrists into the open ends of the forearms and glue.

The goblin in the introductory photograph is handing out rowan berries bound with red thread. These, along with twigs of oak, ash and thorn, are age-old charms to protect the guests from the effects of evil spirits during the meal and on their way home. Take care not to use elder twigs as this tree is sometimes a witch in tree form.

You wouldn't want unexpected guests for dinnner would you?

A PIECE OF CAKE

YOU WILL NEED:
- ☐ Scalpel or modelling knife
- ☐ Scissors
- ☐ Impact adhesive
- ☐ 1 SRA2 sheet of 400gsm cream paper
- ☐ 1 A3 sheet of 80gsm white paper
- ☐ 1 A3 sheet of 80gsm brown paper
- ☐ 1 A3 sheet of 200 gsm pink paper
- ☐ Plenty to decorate your cake with — paint, pens, shiny bits and glittery bits, pink paper etc

The instructions given are for one slice of cake. Six slices make a complete cake of 360mm/14¼in diameter. After drawing out the shapes, but before cutting out the cake, carry out some basic decoration

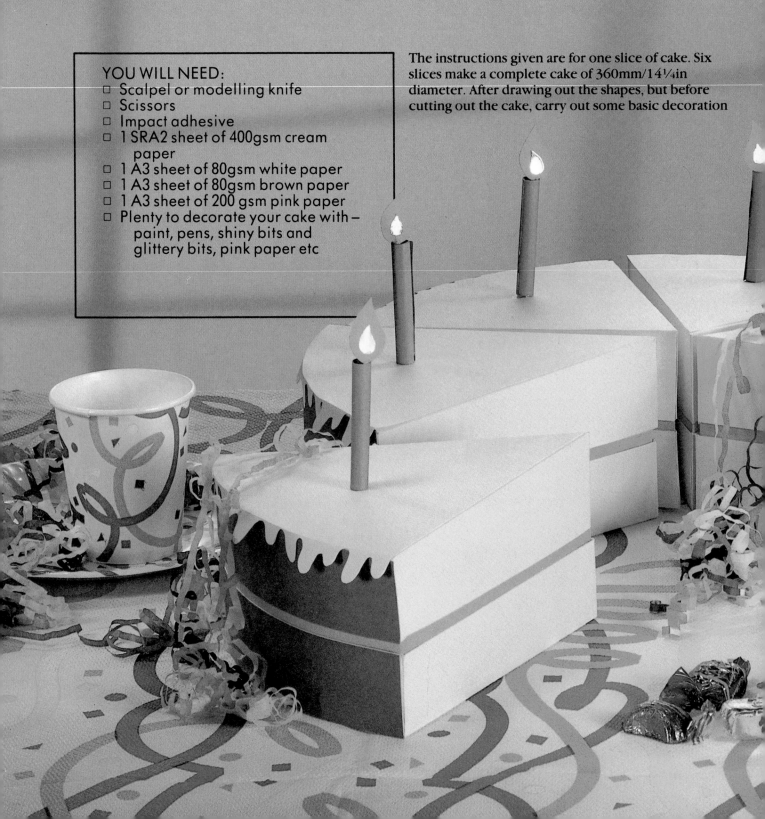

to represent fancy icing. Decoration can be completed on the finished slice.

1 Cut out the top of your cake. Glue 1 to **1**, tabs 2 to **2** and finally 3 to **3**.

2 Cut out the cake bottom, and in an identical way as the top, glue 4 to **4**, tabs 5 to **5** and 6 to 6.

3 Now you have the top and bottom of your cake. To make it open and close as a box, cut out the 'filling' piece from a colour to represent icing. Simply fold along the dotted lines then glue in position inside the cake bottom in the following order 7 to **7**, 8 to **8** and finally 9 to **9**. You now have one slice of cake. Repeat steps 1 – 3 another five times and you will have a complete cake of six slices. You can either decorate each piece the same, or why not have a real dream cake with six completely different flavoured slices? Don't forget to make little paper rolls for candles, using glittery paper as the flame.

Into each slice place lots of surprises; sweets, toys, coins, hats – everything.

■ Grey areas on diagram = apply glue. Decide what size you would like the finished model to be and draw out the pieces, adjusting the scale accordingly.
■ Cut out large pieces with scissors and small pieces with a scalpel or craft knife.
■ Numbered parts join together, e.g. 1 will glue to a second area marked 1. Circled number = apply glue to top of piece, otherwise apply glue to underside.

■ Cut a scrap of shiny paper to enhance the flame.

■ Use a simple roll of paper to form a candle.

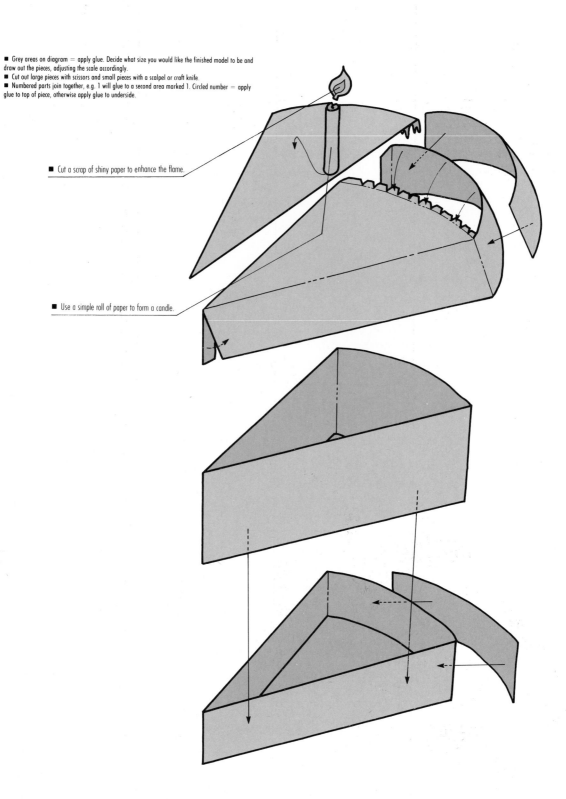

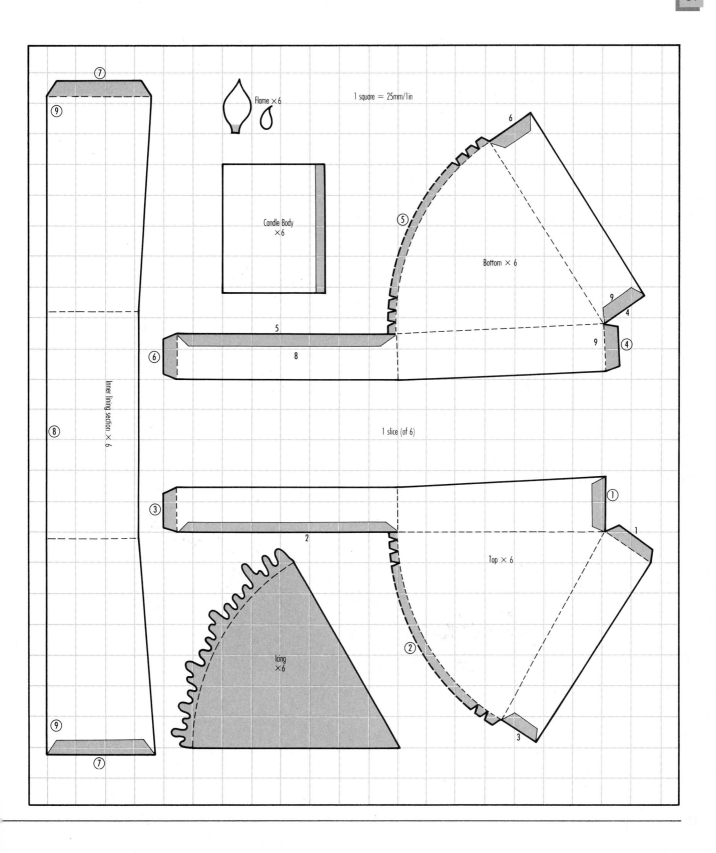

⑦

⑨

Flame × 6

1 square = 25mm/1in

6

Candle Body
× 6

⑤

Bottom × 6

9

4

5

9

4

⑥

8

⑧

Inner lining section × 6

1 slice (of 6)

①

1

③

2

Top × 6

②

Icing
× 6

⑨

3

⑦

CHRISTMAS BOX

As this model incorporates pop-up style moving folds, accurate cutting and folding will make construction considerably easier.

1 Cut out the box section, fold along the dotted lines and glue 1 to **1**, 2 to **2**, 3 to **3** and 4 to **4** to create a simple box structure. The four triangular lid pieces will fold in, to seal the box.

YOU WILL NEED:
- ☐ Scalpel or modelling knife
- ☐ Scissors
- ☐ Impact adhesive
- ☐ 1 A3 sheet of 200gsm yellow paper
- ☐ 7 A4 sheets of 200gsm coloured paper
- ☐ 1 A3 sheet of 200gsm pink paper
- ☐ 1 SRA2 sheet of 400gsm white paper (for the box)

2 The folding inside each lid is identical, so the instructions are for one example, which can be repeated for each of the three remaining lids. Cut out the inner section and glue it inside the box, 5 to **5**.

3 Cut out the division triangle and glue it 6 to **6** to the inner section and 7 to **7** to the inside of the lid.

4 Cut out the folding section. This section can be decorated with colour and glitter, but do not exceed the boundaries of the piece, or the folding will not work. Crease accurately along the dotted lines, and consulting the diagram, fold up. Glue the folding section 8 to **8** and 9 to **9** to the upper side of the inner section.

5 This completes one quarter of the folding mechanism. Repeat instructions 2 to 4 for each remaining lid but join each folding section to its neighbours by gluing 10 to **10**.

6 Carefully fold the folding sections inside the box, so that the top of the box becomes sealed by the lids. Open and close the box several times as this loosens up the folds allowing the model to work more efficiently.

7 To form the paper ribbon, cut out two strips of paper 12mm/½in wide. Form a loop on top of one lid, take the remaining length of paper ribbon down one side of the box, under the base and up the opposite side to form another loop on the facing lid. Cut away any excess. Make sure the loops are firmly glued onto the lids. Repeat this procedure for the remaining two sections. When the box is untied, all the glittery

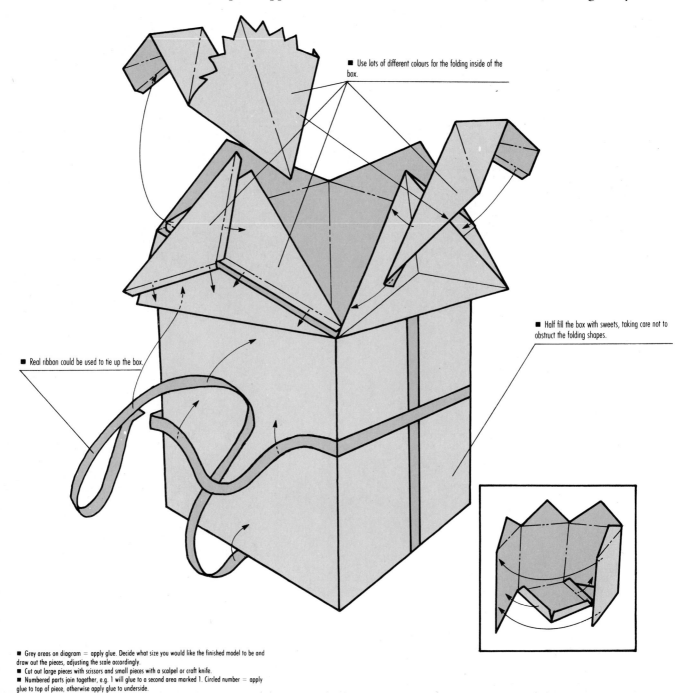

■ Use lots of different colours for the folding inside of the box.

■ Half fill the box with sweets, taking care not to obstruct the folding shapes.

■ Real ribbon could be used to tie up the box.

■ Grey areas on diagram = apply glue. Decide what size you would like the finished model to be and draw out the pieces, adjusting the scale accordingly.
■ Cut out large pieces with scissors and small pieces with a scalpel or craft knife.
■ Numbered parts join together, e.g. 1 will glue to a second area marked 1. Circled number = apply glue to top of piece, otherwise apply glue to underside.

insides of the box fold out into view.

Small gifts, such as sweets, can be inserted into the folds of the box (between the upper surface of the inner section and the folding section) which can then be lifted out and presented to the guests as the box opens. Additional sweets and gifts can be kept in the lower half of the box, but ensure that the free movement of the folds is not inhibited.

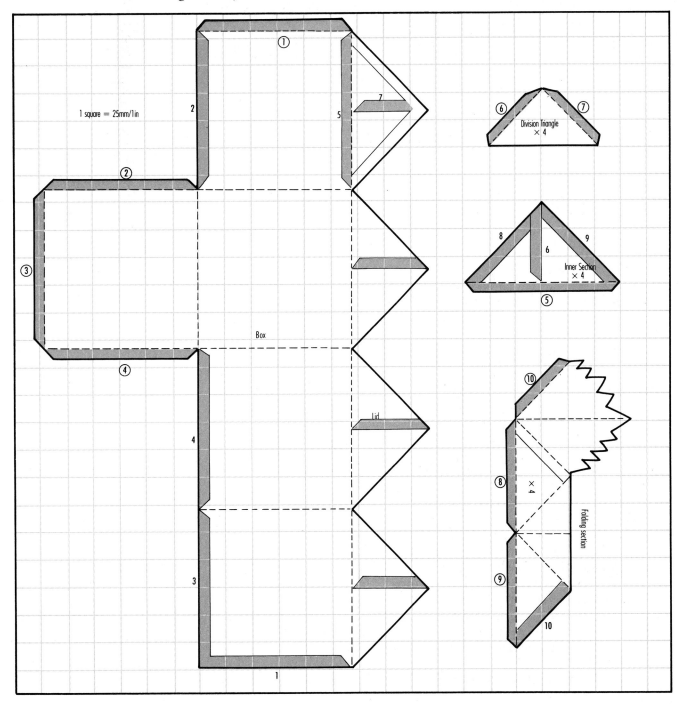

1 square = 25mm/1in

Division Triangle
× 4

Inner Section
× 4

Box

Lid

× 4

Folding section

MOUNT VESUVIUS

The grid dimensions build a 406mm/16in firework.
1 Before cutting out the body cone of the firework, apply any decoration required. Any paper overlays should be firmly stuck down because when

the cone is rolled into shape these may come adrift at the edges. Also cut the slots at the cone summit.
2 Cut out the body cone section. Glue tabs 1 to **1** and

YOU WILL NEED:
- ☐ Scalpel or modelling knife
- ☐ Scissors
- ☐ Impact adhesive
- ☐ 1 SRA2 sheet of 400gsm midnight blue paper
- ☐ 2 SRA2 sheets of 400gsm yellow paper
- ☐ 1 A3 sheet of 80gsm red paper
- ☐ 1 A3 sheet of 80gsm yellow paper
- ☐ 1 A3 sheet of 80gsm orange paper
- ☐ Some scraps of gold and silver foil for the hanging decorations

then seal the cone by gluing body to base, 2 to **2**.

3 Decorate the flames before cutting from the yellow paper, using lots of bright colours.

4 Cut out both the main flame pieces and the four smaller side flames.

5 Take two of the side flames, match and glue the surfaces marked 4. Repeat this step with the two remaining flames.

6 Take the two main flame sections and fold them along the centre to a ninety degree angle. Hold the

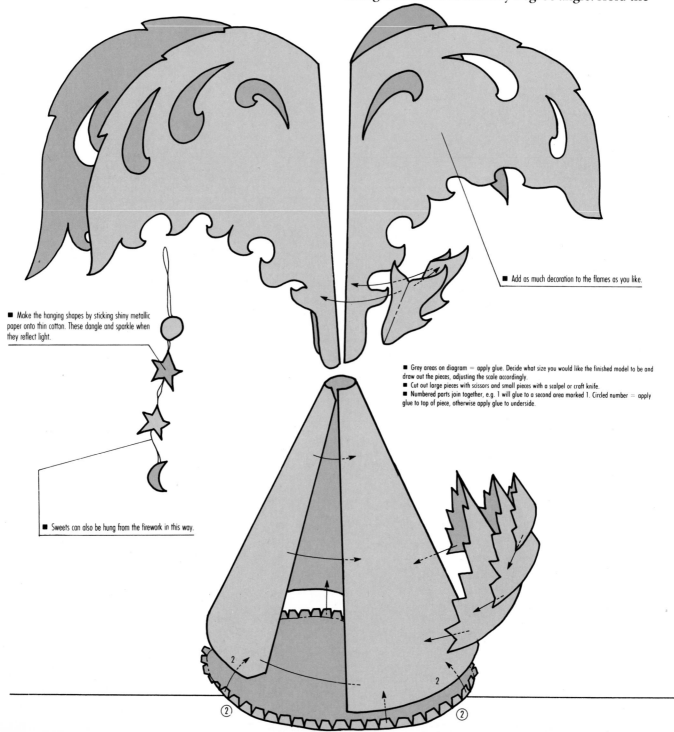

■ Add as much decoration to the flames as you like.

■ Make the hanging shapes by sticking shiny metallic paper onto thin cotton. These dangle and sparkle when they reflect light.

■ Sweets can also be hung from the firework in this way.

■ Grey areas on diagram = apply glue. Decide what size you would like the finished model to be and draw out the pieces, adjusting the scale accordingly.
■ Cut out large pieces with scissors and small pieces with a scalpel or craft knife.
■ Numbered parts join together, e.g. 1 will glue to a second area marked 1. Circled number = apply glue to top of piece, otherwise apply glue to underside.

two main flames centre-fold to centre-fold and notice how they can be joined by positioning the side flames 3 to **3**. Glue the side flames into position.

7 The completed flame section can now be slipped into the summit slots on the cone.

8 The downward-facing flames can be used as hooks from which you can hang threads with glittering stars and coloured shapes to represent falling sparks. These will reflect the light, making the completed model so much more effective.

Side Decoration

Moon

1

1 square = 25mm/1in

Moon

Body

Side flame × 4

4

3

Star

Side Decoration

Side Decoration

½ main flame × 2

3

PAPER POSY

Flower A

1 Cut out the petal base from green paper, and six petals from yellow paper. Form the petal base into a cone by gluing 1 to **1**.

2 One by one, glue the petals into position 2 to **2** inside the petal base. Cut out a second petal base from yellow paper, form it into a cone and slip this inside the green cone, covering up the petal tabs.

3 From yellow paper cut out the trumpet. Score along the dotted line. Gradually curve the trumpet into shape and splay out the ragged edge. Glue 3 to **3**.

4 Glue the trumpet into position at the centre of the flower.

Flower B

5 Cut out the petal from white paper. Score along the dotted line. Roll the petal, folding along the dotted line. Put a line of glue along the lower edge of the petal and roll the petal into shape.

6 Cut out the stamen from yellow paper. Put a dot of glue on the blunt end and slip it into the flower centre.

7 Cut out the flower base from green paper. Form it into a cone by gluing 4 to **4** and glue it into position on the flower.

Flower C

8 Cut out the petal base from green paper, and at least 12 petals from yellow or purple paper. Form the petal base into a cone by gluing 5 to **5**.

9 Glue petals into position, one by one, evenly spacing them around the inside of the petal base. Twelve petals will form a complete circle around the petal base rim. On top of the first line of petals a second row can now be added, each petal positioned mid way between two lower petals. Several rows of petals can be added. When the desired effect is achieved, cut out the yellow or purple flower centre, form it into a cone by gluing 6 to **6**, then place it into position with a spot of glue in the middle of the petals.

Flower D

10 Cut out four red and yellow petals and the base. Glue 7 to **7** in each case, then 8 to **8** of the base, then join and glue all the petals to one another in the base.

11 Cut out the flower centre, glue 8 to **8** and position it in the middle of the petals with a tiny blob of glue.

YOU WILL NEED:
- ☐ Scalpel or modelling knife
- ☐ Scissors
- ☐ Impact adhesive
- ☐ 5 A4 sheets of 200gsm coloured paper, yellow, green, red, white, pink or any other colours
- ☐ 1 A3 sheet of 200gsm green paper
- ☐ Lengths of green wire

Flower E

12 Cut out four blue petals. Score and gently fold along the dotted line. Curve the inside of the petals around a pencil to give them shape. Allow the outside of the petals to fold along the dotted line outwards.

13 Roll the flower base around a pencil, glue 9 to **9**.

Splay the green spiky shapes outwards.

14 Glue each petal into position on the petal base 10 to **10**.

15 Applying a tiny spot of glue carefully attach each petal to its neighbours. The flower can be open or closed depending on how the petals are attached to

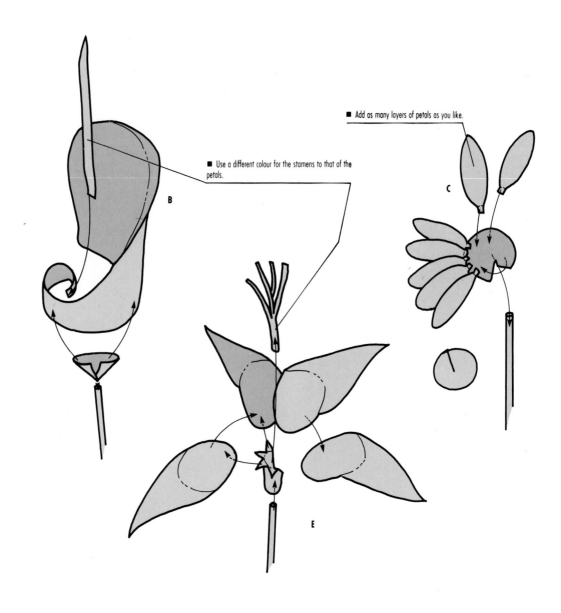

■ Add as many layers of petals as you like.

■ Use a different colour for the stamens to that of the petals.

B

C

E

each other, so for a few moments experiment with the petal positioning.

16 Finally, cut out the yellow stamens. Roll them longways around a pencil, then curve each stamen individually.

Each of the five flowers in this section are variations on simple folding techniques. Many more shapes can easily be developed by altering the size, shape and number of petals. In imitation of real flowers these may be mounted on stems of green wire and arranged in a vase with lots of green paper leaf shapes to represent foliage.

■ Grey areas on diagram = apply glue. Decide what size you would like the finished model to be and draw out the pieces, adjusting the scale accordingly.
■ Cut out large pieces with scissors and small pieces with a scalpel or craft knife.
■ Numbered parts join together, e.g. 1 will glue to a second area marked 1. Circled number = apply glue to top of piece, otherwise apply glue to underside.

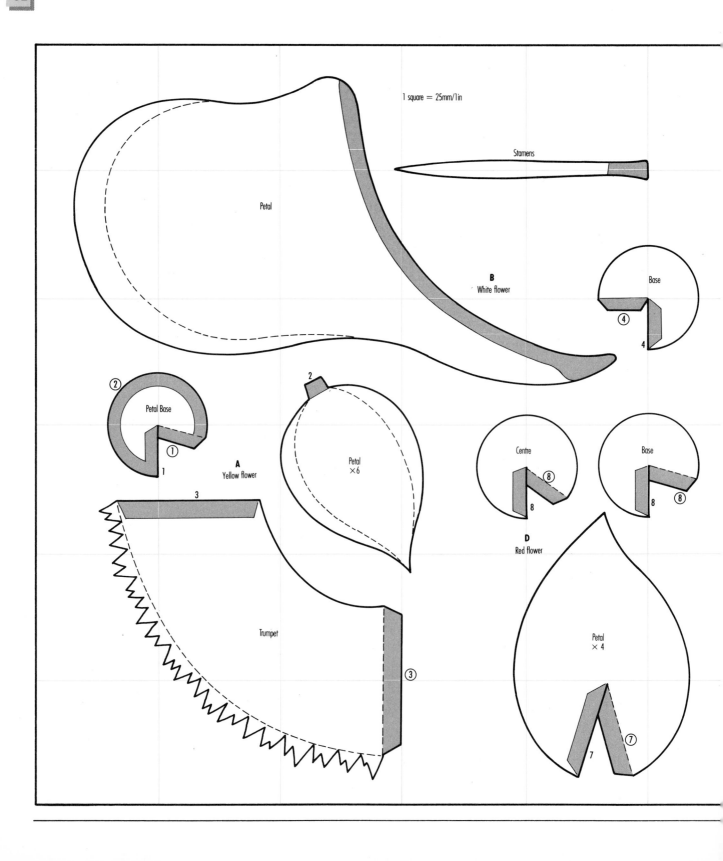

1 square = 25mm/1in

Stamens

Petal

B
White flower

Base
④
4

②
Petal Base
①
1

A
Yellow flower

2
Petal
×6

Centre
⑧
8

Base
8 ⑧

D
Red flower

3

Trumpet

③

Petal
× 4

7
⑦

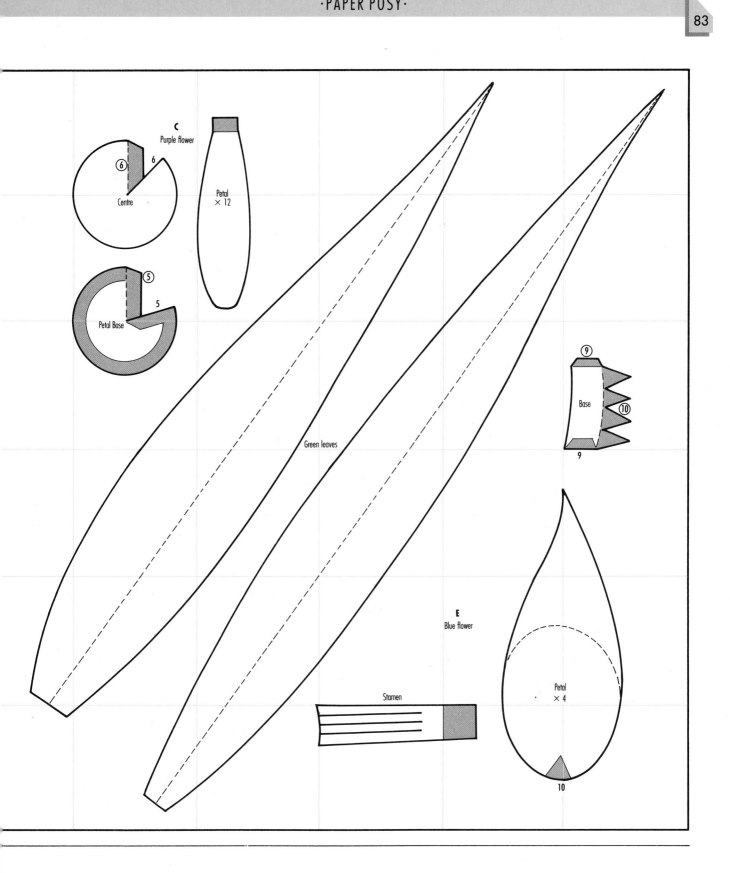

C
Purple flower

⑥ 6

Centre

Petal
× 12

⑤

5

Petal Base

Green leaves

⑨

Base

⑩

9

E
Blue flower

Stamen

Petal
× 4

10

·CHAPTER FOUR·

MAKE A MONSTER

A lot of fun can be had making monsters. People enjoy being frightened by imaginary creatures as so many horror films and books testify. Just spend a few moments contemplating what could be lurking in the darkness of a dense wood or behind the next corner. I find it interesting while working with monster ideas to accept the existence of these weird creatures. The models then become real rather than imaginary, and the only task remaining is to fold the paper into the right shapes.

Late in the film *Aliens* the viewer has come to accept the aliens with their appalling homicidal traits as real. Only when a young girl relates how her mother had assured her that there were no monsters are we reminded that the film is a work of the imagination. But monsters *do* exist, as the girl comes to realize. In my opinion, all those dreadful stories of double-headed, tooth-grinding crazies are probably true and it is time we all got used to the idea!

For this book, however, I have created a group

of harmless looking monsters, based on pre-history. The exception is Robobuggy – a dark and sinister transforming alien from the future.

Paper may seem too domestic a material to encapsulate such violent products of the imagination, but if you substitute varnish for slime, use bizarre colour combinations, and add shiny bits here and there, you can begin to get an idea. It's not so much a question of using one's imagination as not allowing it to be inhibited.

The models here start with a cosy, innocent-looking 'hammerdillo' which is very simple to make and then move on into areas where the modeller can use his or her own imagination for positioning and colouration.

In order of difficulty the section would divide up as hammerdillo, ramphibious, terror dactyl, prickly saurus and finally robobuggy. This last project impinges on the area in which machines cease to know their place in the order of things and begin to develop their own 'natural' history.

I hope this section will spark off a host of weird and wonderful ideas, inspired by half-forgotten dreams and nightmares, fears and obsessions.

You can pursue your own projects. Or maybe they will pursue you . . .

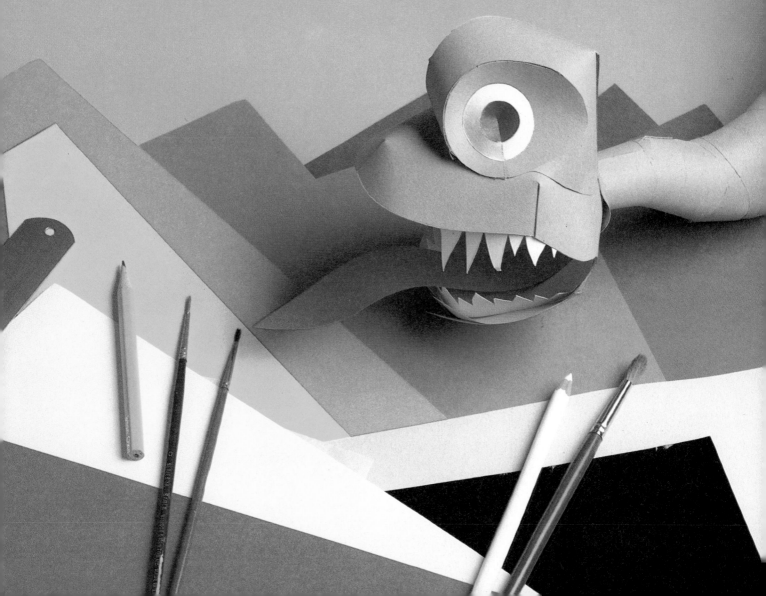

HAMMERDILLO

1 Carefully scale up the model to the required size. The larger the proposed completed model the thicker the paper you will need to use. If the model is to be 304mm/1ft to 609mm/2ft long, 200gsm will be ideal. A 914mm/3ft model or larger will require paper twice as thick.

2 Cut out the body section of the monster. Cut along all the solid lines and score along all the dotted lines.

3 Before gluing it is best to lightly 'pre-fold' along the scored lines.

4 As you fold and glue each flap of the body into position, 1 to **1**, 2 to **2**, 3 to **3** on one side, 4 to **4**, 5 to **5** and 6 to **6** on the other, the shape will magically form itself. Fold and glue tabs 12 to **12** and 13 to **13** to form the indented snout. When you have assembled the body put it to one side and turn your attention to the legs.

5 As with the body, cut along solid lines, fold along dotted lines and before gluing, gently 'pre-fold' along the dotted lines.

6 Assemble the legs, by matching 7 to **7**, 8 to **8**, 9 to **9** and 10 to **10**. The completed leg section simply slots into position on the body.

7 Finally the easiest part of all – cut out the crest and attach this into the slot at the back of the monster's head, 11 to **11**.

Once you have finished the model and found how easy it is, you could make a friend for him from a different coloured paper, as in the photograph. This new model does not, of course, have to be the same size. By varying the scale when enlarging the diagram of the pieces you alter the size of the completed model. The assembly instructions remain the same regardless of the model size.

YOU WILL NEED:
- ☐ Scalpel or modelling knife
- ☐ Scissors
- ☐ Impact adhesive
- ☐ 1 SRA2 sheet of 200gsm green paper
- ☐ Black felt-tipped pen

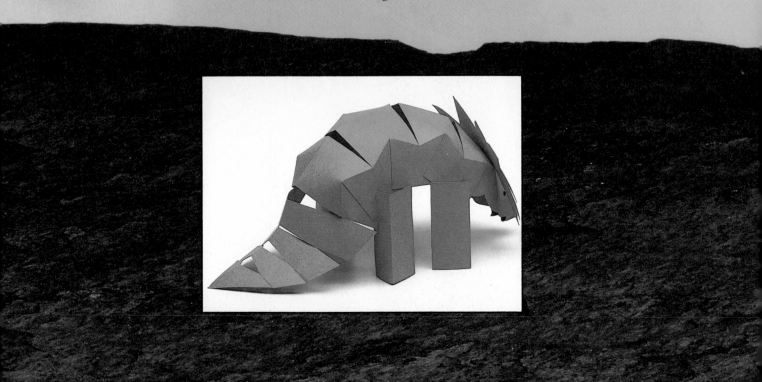

■ Grey areas on diagram = apply glue. Decide what size you would like the finished model to be and draw out the pieces, adjusting the scale accordingly.
■ Cut out large pieces with scissors and small pieces with a scalpel or craft knife.
■ Numbered parts join together, e.g. 1 will glue to a second area marked 1. Circled number = apply glue to top of piece, otherwise apply glue to underside.

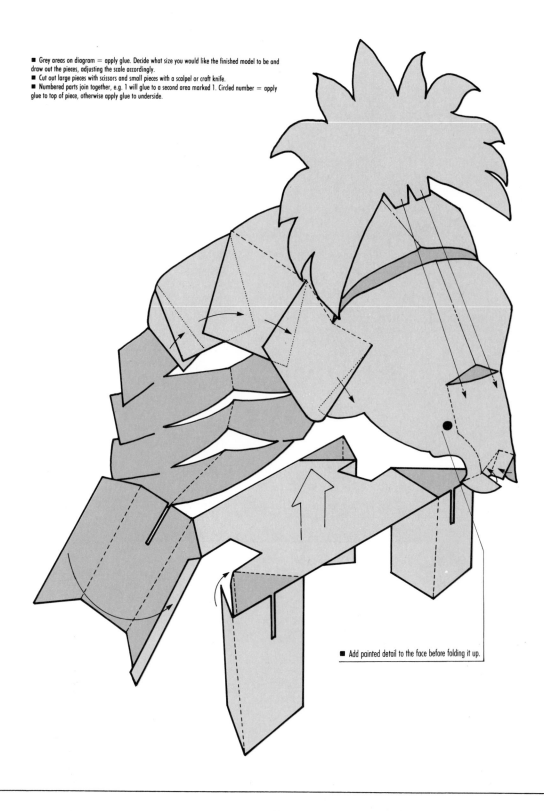

■ Add painted detail to the face before folding it up.

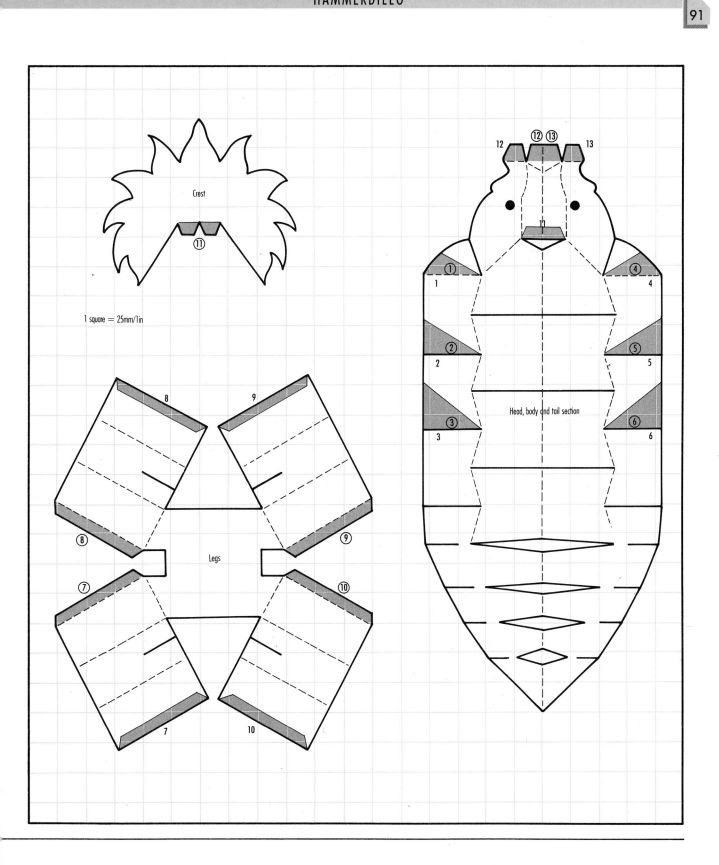

Crest

⑪

1 square = 25mm/1in

8   9

⑧   ⑨

Legs

⑦   ⑩

7   10

12 ⑫ ⑬ 13

11

① 1   ④ 4

② 2   ⑤ 5

Head, body and tail section

③ 3   ⑥ 6

RAMPHIBIOUS

The grid measurement provided builds a 482mm/
19in model. Just think – if it was anything but paper
you could play with it in the bath!

1   Cut out the body section, taking care while cutting
the fin holes. Glue 1 to **1** and 2 to **2**, then tabs 3 to **3**,
tabs 4 to **4** and finally complete the tail 5 to **5**.

2   Turn to the neck. Ten separate pieces go together
to form the neck and there is no fixed method of
joining them, so there can be a degree of flexibility
here, allowing several models to be built, all with
different snake-like necks. Start by gluing the separate
sections to form ten rings 6 to **6**, 7 to **7**, 8 to **8** etc.
The rings – a more accurate description is cones with
the point cut off – go one on top of the other, fat

YOU WILL NEED:
- □ Scalpel or modelling knife
- □ Scissors
- □ Impact adhesive
- □ 3 SRA2 sheets of 200gsm blue paper
- □ 1 SRA2 sheet of 80gsm pink paper
- □ Some scraps of bright red 80gsm paper (tongue) and white, yellow or cream paper (teeth)
- □ Paint and pens for any detail you may wish to add

end to thin each time until a curvy snake-like form is created. Before permanently gluing the neck just play around for a few minutes experimentally, seeing just what can be achieved. When a shape is decided upon, glue the neck together and complete the structure by cutting out the head support ring and gluing 9 to **9** to the thin end of the neck.

3 Cut out the eyes and forehead piece. Carefully score and make up each eye – study the diagram and

photograph for guidance on the completed shape. Glue tabs 10 to **10** on the right eye and 11 to **11** on the left. Form the forehead by assembling tabs 12 to **12**, 13 to **13** and 13A to **13A**.

4 While this is all drying turn your attention to the jaws. Before cutting the jaws, line the blue paper with pink paper. Cut out the upper jaw. Glue tabs 14 to **14**. Cut out the lower jaw and in the same way glue tabs 15 to **15**. Join the two jaws by gluing 16 to **16**.

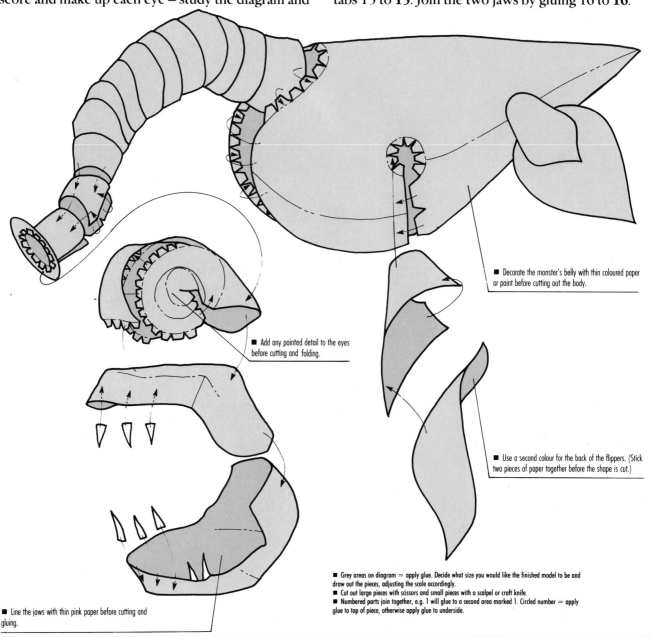

■ Decorate the monster's belly with thin coloured paper or paint before cutting out the body.

■ Add any painted detail to the eyes before cutting and folding.

■ Use a second colour for the back of the flippers. (Stick two pieces of paper together before the shape is cut.)

■ Grey areas on diagram = apply glue. Decide what size you would like the finished model to be and draw out the pieces, adjusting the scale accordingly.
■ Cut out large pieces with scissors and small pieces with a scalpel or craft knife.
■ Numbered parts join together, e.g. 1 will glue to a second area marked 1. Circled number = apply glue to top of piece, otherwise apply glue to underside.

■ Line the jaws with thin pink paper before cutting and gluing.

5 Glue the eye and forehead section onto the upper jaw by attaching tabs 17 to **17** and then 18 to **18**. Also adhere the base of each eye to the jaw and make a snug fit.

6 Stick the tongue into the mouth and curve it randomly to make your monster as lively as possible. Also fill its mouth with many sharp, crooked, vicious teeth. These might be best made from cream or even yellow paper as I do not think sea monsters brush their teeth too often!

7 Glue the completed head onto the thin end of the neck. The head support ring allows you to use plenty of glue here for extra strength.

8 Mount the neck on the body by gluing tabs 19 to **19**.

9 To assemble each fin, glue 20 to **20** and 21 to **21**.

10 Finally join each fin one at a time to the body by applying glue to tabs 23 and slipping the end of each fin into the hole in the body.

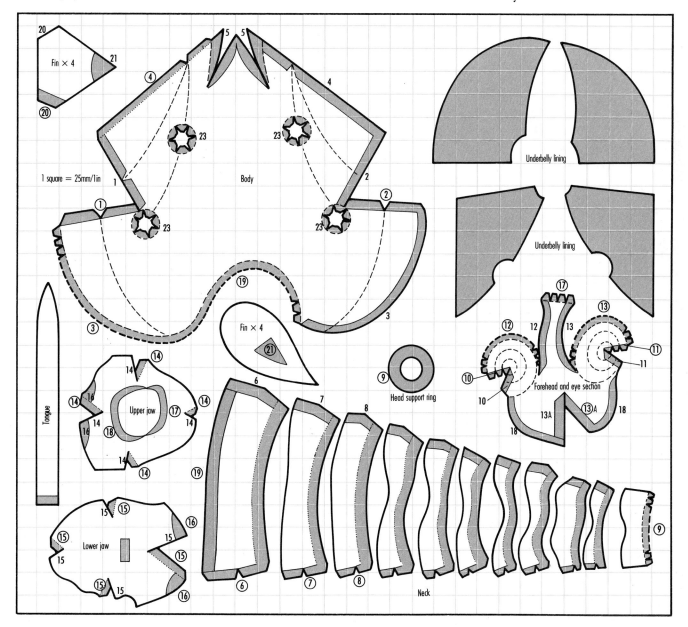

TERROR DACTYL

The grid measurement provided will build a huge monster with a 1m/3ft 4in wingspan.

1 Begin by cutting out the body section. Glue tabs 1 to **1**, then tabs 2 to **2**, 3 to **3** and finally 4 to **4**.

2 Cut out the five pieces that form the neck. When 5 to **5**, 6 to **6**, 7 to **7**, 8 to **8** and 9 to **9** are glued you will have five rings, or more accurately five cones with the points cut off. This method of forming the neck allows a great deal of flexibility in creating the final shape. Before permanent assembly, spend a few minutes experimentally joining the rings fat end to thin end and discover the variety of writhing shapes that can be achieved. When a satisfactorily strange combination is discovered, glue permanently.

3 Glue the tabs on the end of the neck to the head support ring 10 to **10**.

4 Cut out the eye and forehead section. Carefully score the eyes and, using the diagram and photograph for guidance, assemble the eyes. Hold firm by gluing 11 to **11** and 12 to **12**.

5 Score along the dotted lines on the forehead but do not attempt to fold now. For once this is easiest to

YOU WILL NEED:
- Scalpel or modelling knife
- Scissors
- Impact adhesive
- 4 SRA2 sheets of 200gsm mauve paper for the body, neck, head, arms, legs, wings, hands and feet
- 1 SRA2 sheet of 80gsm yellow paper for the underbelly
- 1 SRA2 sheet of 80gsm pink paper for the inside of the monster's mouth
- Some scraps of red and white for the tongue and fangs
- Paint and pens to tint the eyes

achieve on the completed head. To form the forehead, glue tabs 13 to **13**, 14 to **14** and 15 to **15**.

6 While this is drying, line each jaw with pink paper for the mouth interior. Cut out the upper and lower jaw. Assemble each of them by gluing 16 to **16** on the upper jaw and 17 to **17** on the lower. Gently fold along the scored lines to give more shape, then join the two jaws together 18 to **18**.

7 Cut out the two sections that form the horn. Score and gently curve into shape each piece then glue 19 to **19**.

8 Apply glue to the tabs 20 on the eye and forehead section and at **20** on the horn. Gently push the horn into position and allow to become firm before continuing.

9 Join the eye and forehead section to the upper jaw by gluing tabs 21 to **21** and 22 to **22**. Also apply glue to the base of each eye to make the join as snug as possible. When this has dried gently push in the scored lines between the eyes.

10 Curve the tongue into a vigorously lashing shape and stick it into the mouth. Also cut many jagged, ferocious teeth and stick them into the mouth.

11 Adhere the completed head to the head support ring. Use plenty of glue to give a good firm join.

12 Cut out the upper and lower arm. Join 23 to **23** and 24 to **24** then attach the two pieces together by gluing tabs 25 to **25**. Apply glue to tabs 26 on the body section and **26** on the arm. Slip the end of each arm into the body and allow to become firm before continuing.

13 Cut out each wing. Glue to the body 27 to **27** and glue the leading edge onto the arm 28 to **28**.

14 Glue the hands in position at the end of each arm 29 to **29**.

15 Cut out the pieces that form the upper and lower legs. Glue 30 to **30** and 31 to **31**. Join the upper and lower legs by gluing tabs 32 to **32**.

16 When both right and left legs are completed join

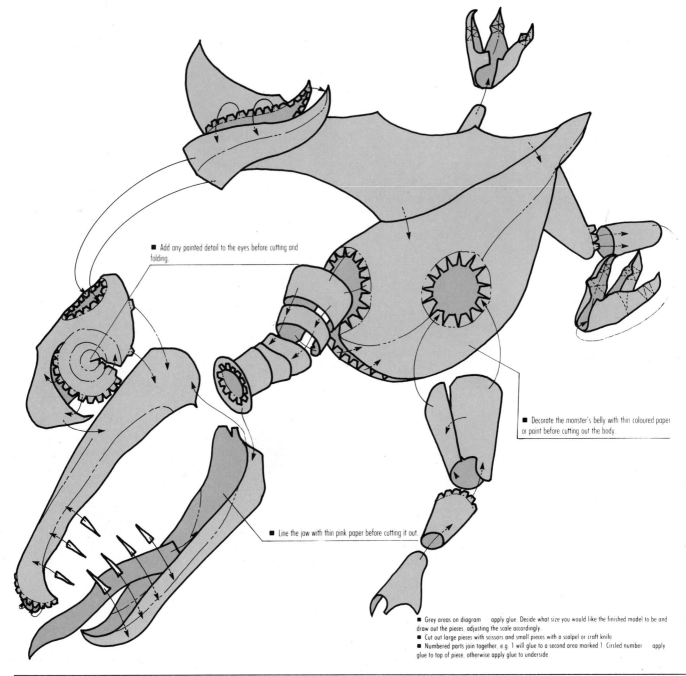

■ Add any painted detail to the eyes before cutting and folding.

■ Decorate the monster's belly with thin coloured paper or paint before cutting out the body.

■ Line the jaw with thin pink paper before cutting it out.

■ Grey areas on diagram   apply glue. Decide what size you would like the finished model to be and draw out the pieces, adjusting the scale accordingly.
■ Cut out large pieces with scissors and small pieces with a scalpel or craft knife.
■ Numbered parts join together, e.g. 1 will glue to a second area marked 1. Circled number   apply glue to top of piece, otherwise apply glue to underside.

them together by gluing tabs 33 to **33**.

17 Glue completed legs onto the wings and body 34 to **34**.

18 Finally cut out each foot. Score and fold along the dotted lines then glue 35 to **35** and pinch each claw together and glue 36 to **36** in each case. To complete the monster glue each foot onto the tip of each leg 37 to **37**.

The terror dactyl can be displayed by looping thread under each wing and suspending from the ceiling – he may be a bit overweight to hang from light fittings.

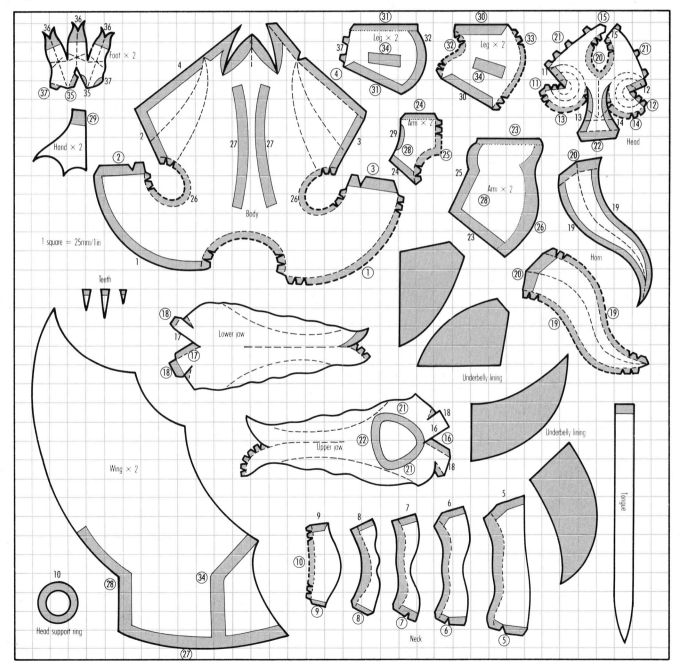

PRICKLY SAURUS

YOU WILL NEED:
- ☐ Scalpel or modelling knife
- ☐ Scissors
- ☐ Impact adhesive
- ☐ 4 SRA2 sheets of 200gsm rust/ brown paper
- ☐ 2 SRA2 sheets of 200gsm cream paper
- ☐ Some scraps of white and red for teeth and tongue
- ☐ Paint or felt-tipped pens for details (eyes etc)

The grid measurement provided builds a monster 1m/3ft 4in long. It is also pretty fat, altogether a large-scale monster.

1 Cut out all four body sections from rust/brown paper. Cut out the hole in section 1 as this makes assembly considerably easier – it can always be sealed later. Take the strips (sections 3 and 4) and glue to section 1, 1 to **1**, 2 to **2**. Join 3 to **3** and 4 to **4** on

section 2 to give it a dome-like appearance, and then glue to sections 1, 3 and 4 (1 to **1**), (2 to **2**). This is where the hole in section 1 becomes rather useful. You can insert your hand to apply the required pressure on the tabs.

2 Put aside the body shell and cut out the eight pieces that form the tail. By gluing 5 to **5**, 6 to **6**, 7 to **7**, 8 to **8**, 9 to **9**, 10 to **10**, 11 to **11**, and 12 to **12**, you will have created a series of rings, or more accurately cones with the points cut off. This method of forming the tail allows a great deal of flexibility in creating the final shape. Before permanent assembly, spend a few minutes experimentally joining the rings fat end to thin end and discover the variety of twisting shapes that can be achieved. When a suitably strange combination is discovered glue permanently.

3 Cut out the three club tail pieces. Create two cones by gluing 13 to **13** and 14 to **14**. Join the two cones together with the strip (section 3) by gluing 15 to **15** and 16 to **16**. By applying glue to tabs 17 the tail can be completed by slipping the club onto the tail tip 17 to **17**.

4 With all the practice gained in producing the tail, building your monster's neck should be child's play; it is the same principle of joining cones together. Once again before final gluing, a better effect will be achieved by experimentally assembling the individual pieces first. After the final shape is decided upon and

glued, attach the head support ring 18 to **18**.

5 Attach the tail to the body shell 19 to **19**. Once again the hole in the body underside will be indispensable in gaining access to apply pressure. Employing the same technique, place the neck into position 20 to **20**.

6 Two pieces form each leg. Start by cutting out the

four pieces to make the two front legs. Score the semi-circles on the foot and gently fold along them. Make the foot by gluing 21 to **21**. Fold in the 'nails' (the previously scored semi-circles) and, using scissors, trim them so that the foot rests evenly on a flat surface.

7 Make the leg by gluing 22 to **22**. Join the foot to the

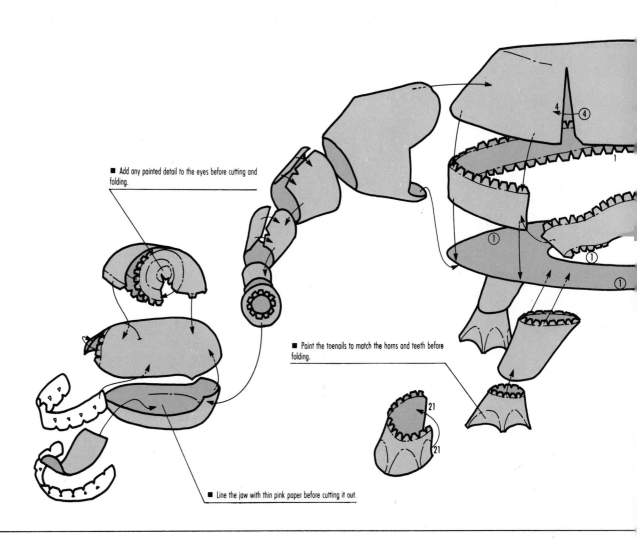

■ Add any painted detail to the eyes before cutting and folding.

■ Paint the toenails to match the horns and teeth before folding.

■ Line the jaw with thin pink paper before cutting it out.

leg by gluing tabs 23 to **23**.

8 Repeat steps 6 and 7 for the three remaining legs. Make sure you attach the correct foot to each leg (the back legs differ slightly from the front).

9 By folding in tabs 24 and applying glue to the upper surface, the legs can be joined to the body shell.

10 Cut out the eye and forehead section. Score the circles of the eyes and gently mould into shape consulting the diagram and photograph for guidance.

11 To create the forehead glue tabs 25 to **25** and 26 to **26**.

12 While this is drying, line the jaws with pink paper. Now cut out the upper and lower jaws. Assemble

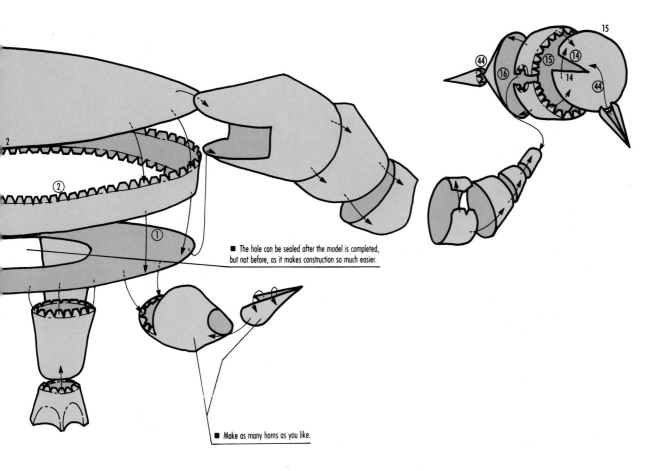

■ The hole can be sealed after the model is completed, but not before, as it makes construction so much easier.

■ Make as many horns as you like.

■ Grey areas on diagram = apply glue. Decide what size you would like the finished model to be and draw out the pieces, adjusting the scale accordingly.

■ Cut out large pieces with scissors and small pieces with a scalpel or craft knife.

■ Numbered parts join together, e.g. 1 will glue to a second area marked 1. Circled number = apply glue to top of piece, otherwise apply glue to underside.

these by gluing tabs 27 to **27**, 28 to **28** in the upper jaw and 29 to **29**, 30 to **30** in the lower jaw. Ensure that the slot in the upper jaw is cut. Join the two jaws by gluing 31 to **31**.

13 Join the eye and forehead section to the upper jaw by slipping tabs 32 into the slot and gluing inside the jaw, and glue tabs 33 to **33**.

14 Put your monster's dentures in now by gluing 34 to **34**, 35 to **35** in the lower jaw and 36 to **36**, 37 to 37 in the upper. Complete the monster's head by attaching a curvy tongue, cut from red paper.

15 Glue the head to the head support ring on the neck.

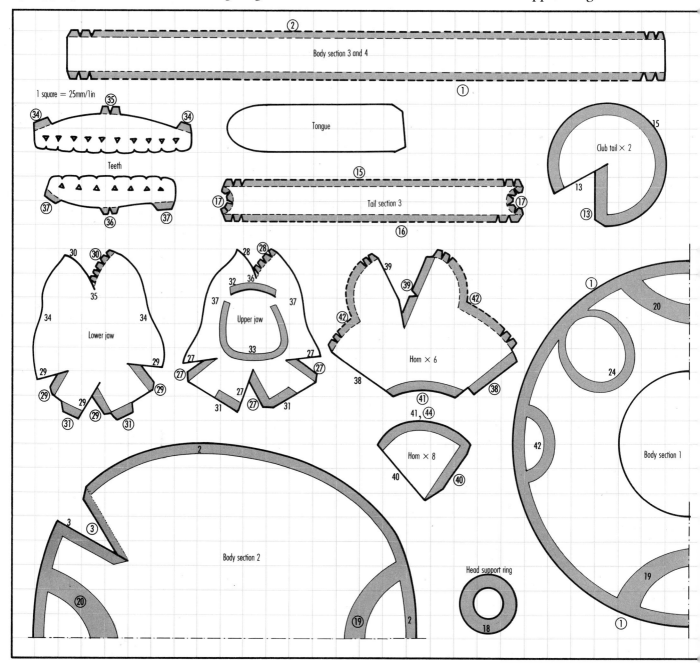

16 Now cut out the pieces to make horns for your monster. There are two kinds of horn, large, with an underside for attachment to the body shell, and shorter ones for attachment to the club. Glue **38** to 38, **39** to 39, **40** to 40 and **41** to 41 to form the large horns, then fold in tabs 42, apply glue to the outer

surface and glue to the body shell.

17 To build the shorter horns, simply glue 40 to **40**. Attach these to the club by folding in tabs **44**. Apply glue to the outer surface and stick into place.

Leave your prickly saurus on the floor in ill-lit corners and see the effect on your cat!

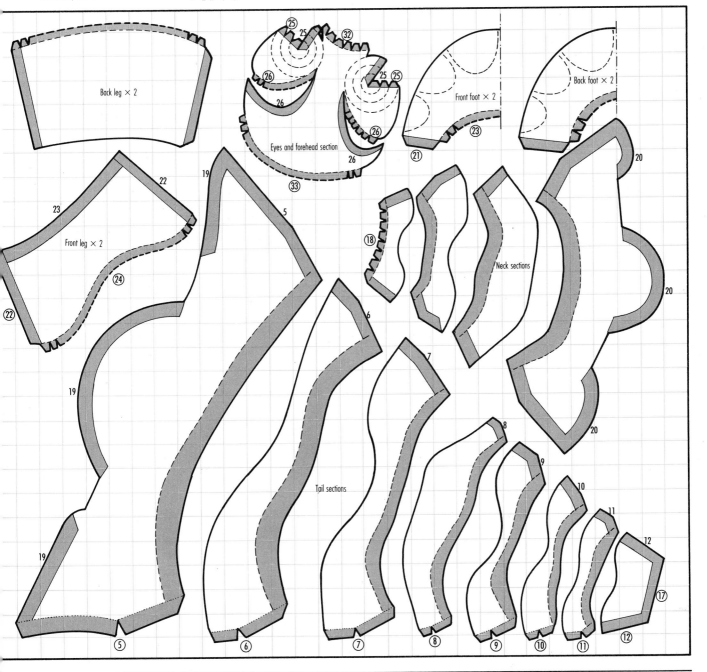

ROBOBUGGY

The grid measurement provided builds a Robobuggy
381mm/15in long.

1 Begin by cutting out the three carriage sections.
Section 2 should be cut from the white paper chosen
for the machine's interior. Score and fold section 3
along the dotted lines then glue 1 to **1**, 2 to **2** and 3 to
3. Complete section 3 by gluing 4 to **4** and 5 to **5**.
Take section 3 and join to section 2 by gluing 6 to **6**, 7
to **7**, 8 to **8**, 9 to **9**, 10 to **10**, 11 to **11**, 12 to **12** and 13
to **13**. This is made easier by folding all the tabs on
section 3 inwards, applying glue to the upper surface
and the lower edges of section 2 then gently lowering
section 2 into position. Take carriage section 1. Glue
14 to **14**, 15 to **15**, 16 to **16** and 17 to **17** where
indicated. Make small '×' shaped incisions into this
piece for the axles, just large enough for a straw to be
pushed through. Complete the carriage by gluing 18
to **18**, 19 to **19**, 20 to **20** and 21 to **21**. Once again,
this is easiest if the tabs on section 1 are folded
inwards and the upper surface coated with glue.

2 Cut out the three head sections. Apply glue to tabs
22 on section 3 and join to section 1. In the same way
apply glue to tabs 23 on section 3 and join to section
2. Finally glue tabs 24 on 1 to section 2.

3 Cut out all the pieces that form the wheels (wheel
backs, wheel hubs and wheel rims). Form the wheel
hubs by scoring and gently folding along the dotted
lines. Refer to the diagram and illustration for
guidance. Glue 25 to **25**. Glue the wheel hub to the
rim 26 to **26** then position the wheel back 27 to **27**.
Work in the same way to complete all four wheels.

4 Two drinking straws are used to make the axles.
Take one, cut it to size and split the ends. Using a
small amount of sticky tape, secure one straw to the
centre of a wheel back by parting the split end of the
straw and attaching each half. To neaten the join
apply glue to one side of a strengthening circle and
slip (glue face down) along the straw to cover the
join.

5 Cut out an axle support. Slip the straw through the
centre hole and glue 28 to **28** and 29 to **29**. You now
have one axle with a wheel at one end. Attach the
second straw to another wheel using the same
technique.

YOU WILL NEED:
- Scalpel or modelling knife
- Scissors
- Impact adhesive
- 2 SRA2 sheets of 200gsm shiny black paper
- 2 SRA2 sheets of 200gsm pearly white paper
- 2 drinking straws

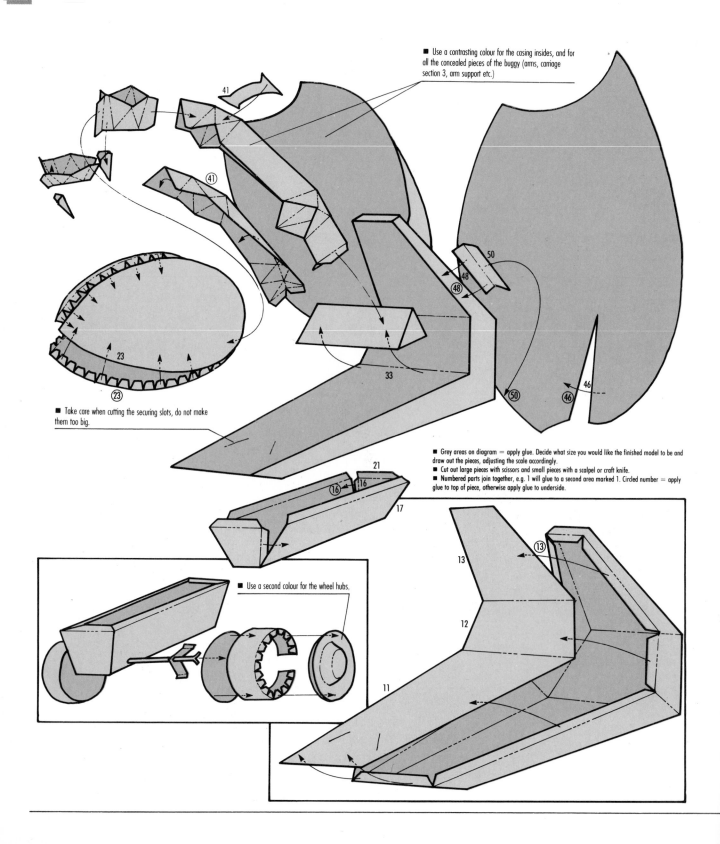

■ Use a contrasting colour for the casing insides, and for all the concealed pieces of the buggy (arms, carriage section 3, arm support etc.)

41

41

50

48

48

23

23

33

50

46

46

■ Take care when cutting the securing slots, do not make them too big.

■ Grey areas on diagram = apply glue. Decide what size you would like the finished model to be and draw out the pieces, adjusting the scale accordingly.
■ Cut out large pieces with scissors and small pieces with a scalpel or craft knife.
■ Numbered parts join together, e.g. 1 will glue to a second area marked 1. Circled number = apply glue to top of piece, otherwise apply glue to underside.

21

16   16

17

13

13

12

11

■ Use a second colour for the wheel hubs.

6 Obviously, before the second wheel can be attached to each axle the axle must be pushed through carriage section 1. This is easily done as you will have made ✕-shaped incisions for this purpose.

7 Before attempting to secure the remaining wheels do not forget to slip an axle support and a strengthening circle onto each wheel first. Joining the last two wheels is trickier than the first two as space is tighter but it is virtually the same operation as before. (See steps 4 and 5).

8 Cut out the arm support. Glue 30 to **30**, 31 to **31** and 32 to **32**. Position this piece at the rear of the carriage and secure 33 to **33**.

9 Cut out one arm from the white paper used for the interior. A special fold has been employed here to allow the arms to move when the model is completed, so take care whilst assembling these parts to achieve the best effect. Score along the dotted lines. On section 1 glue 34 to **34** and 35 to **35** but fold out tabs taking care not to join them. Work in a similar way on section 2 gluing 36 to **36**, 37 to **37** and 38 to **38**. While gluing these slip section 1 into position. Pay careful attention to the diagram as you assemble these pieces. You will find that the

completed arm will bend and twist in all directons, as the folding process allows a great deal of movement.
10 Repeat step 9 for the second arm.
11 Glue the arms in position on the arm support, 39 to **39**. (This piece has previously been attached to the carriage).

12 To provide more strength and unity in arm movement, position and glue the arm link 40 to **40** and 41 to **41**.
13 Now place the head into position at the end of the arms 42 to **42**.
14 To prevent the arms pushing the head forward too

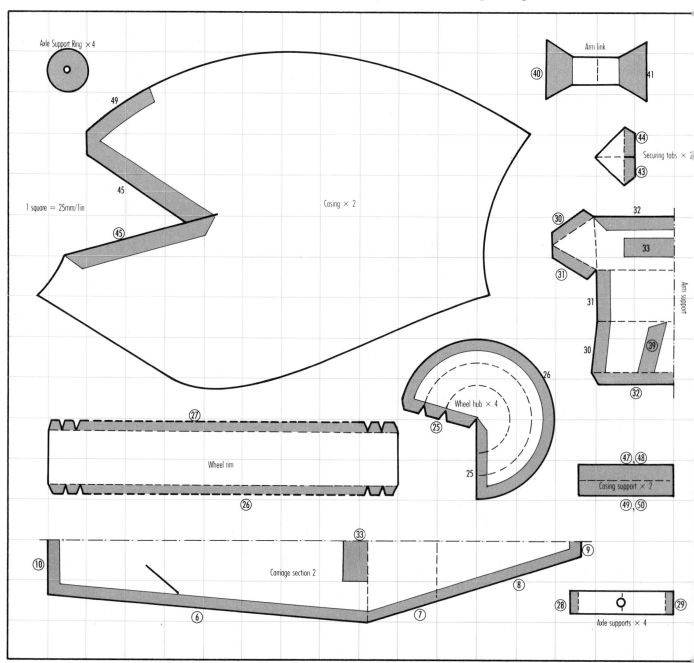

much, and to give the head some stability whilst at rest, the securing tabs should be glued into position 43 to **43** and 44 to **44**. These tabs slip into the slots on the carriage.

15 Before cutting out the casing sections, line the inside with the white paper. Glue 45 to **45** 46 to **46**.

16 Cut the case supports for the paper to match the inside of your model. Glue one side to the case 47 to **47** and 48 to **48**.

17 Each case can now be secured to the carriage by gluing 49 to **49** and 50 to **50**. The best effect will be achieved by trial positioning before the final gluing.

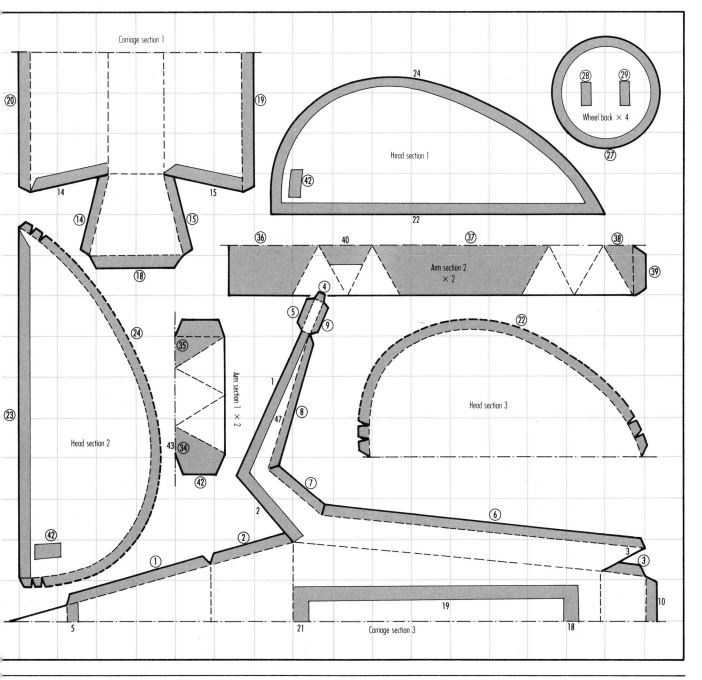

DESK-TOP DESIGNS

The ideas and constructions in this section are quite varied. Each toy is meant to fulfil a useful function, but also to be novel and amusing. Movement is involved in all the models, and therein lies the appeal to jaded, sedentary office workers.

While developing this section my imagination often spiralled and I became very involved in designing weird contraptions which performed all kinds of strange operations, but I baulked at the thought of laying out some of these machines and attempting to explain, in any coherent way, their construction. For me the problem was combining movement and interest with a useful function, yet also ensuring that the models were reasonably simple to assemble.

The easiest project in the section is the pop-up bugging device, followed, in order of difficulty, by the pen pusher, the paddle steamer, the pyramid puzzle and finally the crying wolf. You may question my saying that the pyramid puzzle is second most difficult, but try it and all will be revealed! While working on this model I became convinced I fully understood how I was going to assemble it but then I would hesitate and find myself completely confused. I discovered a couple of variations on this theme, and was again amazed at the complexities of seemingly simple three-dimensional objects.

Victorian and Edwardian tin-plate toys were at the forefront of my mind when working on the pen pusher traction engine and the paddle steamer. Browsing through picture books on this subject is an unfailing source of ideas. The talent of those past toymakers is unsurpassed, but often paper can be a frustrating material to work with if you are trying to realize the more bizarre ideas involving movement. I have made quite complex working models in materials that really should never be expected to fulfil such a function. It can

be a painstaking operation demanding a great deal of patience. Models that *must* work refuse to oblige – for mystifying reasons. The traction engine and paddle steamer, however, should not be quite so demanding.

The crying wolf is a domestic gargoyle. (Tissues are a little less violent than boiling oil, and rather more useful to have on a desk top.) This model is one of the most difficult in the collection, as it requires a more sculptural way of working, and more cuts and tucks to build the form. If you accomplish this without too many problems – no violent tantrums resulting in screwed-up prototypes flying at speed towards your nonplussed cat – you should be ready to develop completely original projects with which to litter your office, or to give away to colleagues.

BUGGING DEVICE

YOU WILL NEED:
- ☐ Scalpel or modelling knife
- ☐ Scissors
- ☐ Impact adhesive
- ☐ Notepad, which opens like a book
- ☐ 1 A4 sheet of 400gsm black paper
- ☐ 1 sheet of 400gsm green paper for the base board which will need to be as big as an open double-page spread of the notepad.
- ☐ Some scraps of yellow paper for decoration
- ☐ Red adhesive 'spots'
- ☐ White paint and a pen to tint the eyes

The size of the insect you are going to make can be varied to fit the size of your notepad. The height and width of the base board shape provided here are the minimum to conceal the folded insect. Obviously the glue points for the feet must not be changed, but the overall dimensions of the base board can be altered to correspond to the page size of your notepad.

1   Cut out the base board, and crease along the central dotted line.

2   Cut out each leg section. Crease along the dotted lines and then carefully stick each foot in place on the base board 1 to **1**, 6 to **6**, 2 to **2**, 5 to **5**, 4 to 4, 3 to **3**. Finally join all the legs together at the centre point 7 to **7** and 8 to **8**.

3 Cut out the bug body and slot it onto the legs parallel to the centre line of the base board. The complete pop-up bug can now be inserted into the front page of the notepad to spring out at unsuspecting readers.

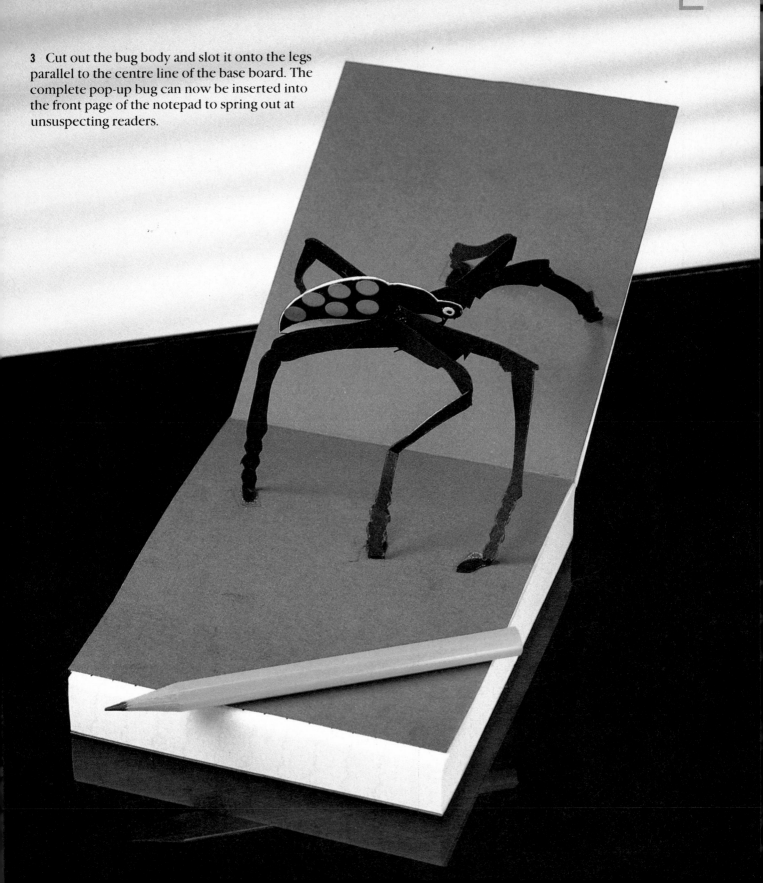

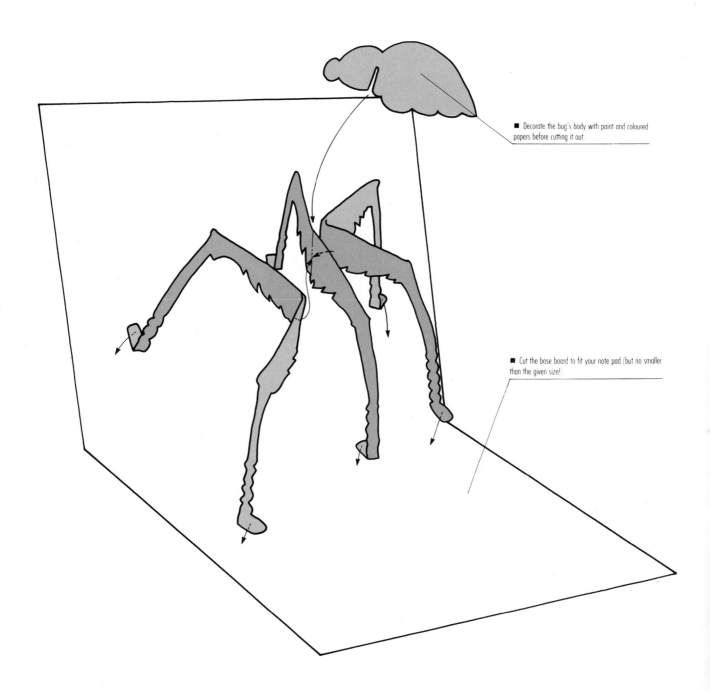

■ Decorate the bug's body with paint and coloured papers before cutting it out.

■ Cut the base board to fit your note pad (but no smaller than the given size!)

■ Grey areas on diagram   apply glue. Decide what size you would like the finished model to be and draw out the pieces, adjusting the scale accordingly.
■ Cut out large pieces with scissors and small pieces with a scalpel or craft knife.
■ Numbered parts join together, e.g. 1 will glue to a second area marked 1. Circled number   apply glue to top of piece, otherwise apply glue to underside.

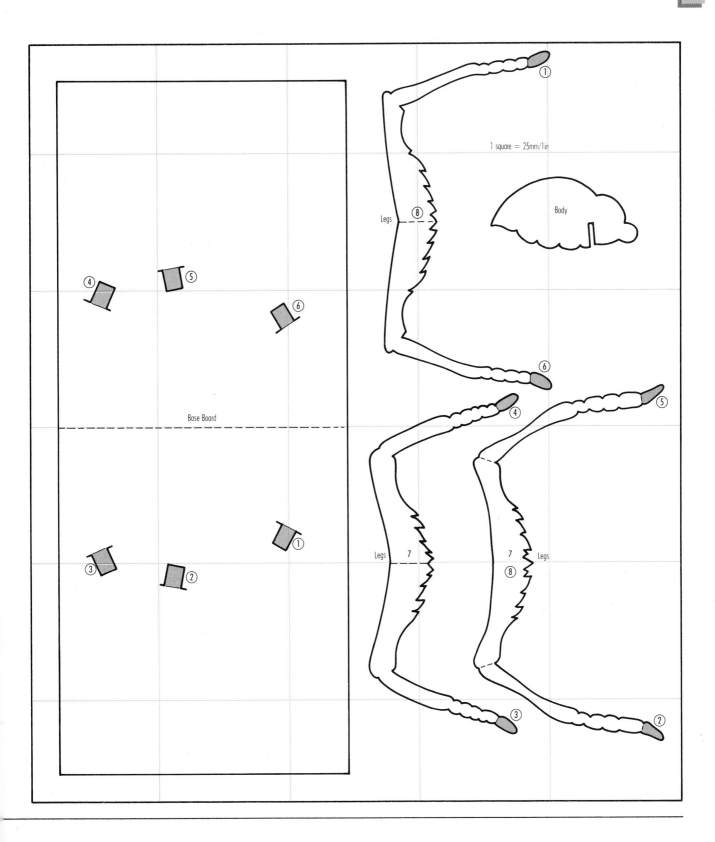

1 square = 25mm/1in

Body

Legs ⑧

⑥

④

⑤

Base Board

①

③

②

Legs 7

7 Legs

⑧

③

②

PAPERCLIP PYRAMID

The grid measurement provided makes up into a pyramid 110mm/4¼in high.

1 Cut out section 2. Glue 1 to **1**, 2 to **2**, and 3 to **3** to form a complete triangular pyramid (or tetrahedron). While accomplishing this observe the principle of the construction as it will be invaluable experience as section 1 is tackled.

2 Cut out section 1 and crease along the dotted lines. Gently fold along these lines to loosen them.

3 One by one, carefully match the numbers to each other, 2 to **2**, 3 to **3** and 1 to **1**. Move on to 9 to **9**, 10 to **10** and come back to join 8 to **8**. Each of these stages forms an extra pyramid. Complete 11 to **11**, 12 to **12** and 13 to **13**. Join 7 to **7**. This does not form a pyramid but lends more solidity to the design. Glue 5 to **5** but leave 4 to 4 and 6 to 6 unglued so that it forms a 'secret' box.

4 Attach section 2 to 1 by gluing 14 to **14**.

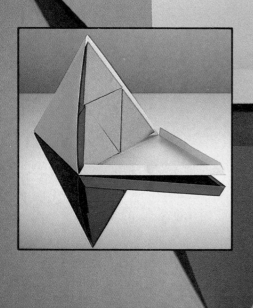

5 Line the gold paper with the pink. Allow them to dry, then cut out section 3. Glue 15 to **15** but again leave the other tabs unglued so this pyramid fits inside the secret chamber.

6 Cut out section 4. Glue 16 to **16**. By leaving the other two tabs unglued this provides the pyramid box into which all the other pieces fit. Once the gold pyramid is filled with paperclips and slipped into the secret chamber, the attached sections 1 and 2 fold into a pyramid that fits comfortably into section 4.

Hand this to the next person to bother you for a paperclip and be confident that you will not be disturbed in the forseeable future!

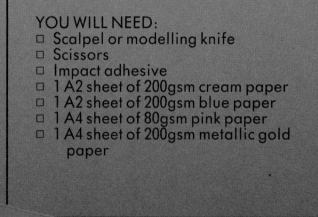

YOU WILL NEED:
- □ Scalpel or modelling knife
- □ Scissors
- □ Impact adhesive
- □ 1 A2 sheet of 200gsm cream paper
- □ 1 A2 sheet of 200gsm blue paper
- □ 1 A4 sheet of 80gsm pink paper
- □ 1 A4 sheet of 200gsm metallic gold paper

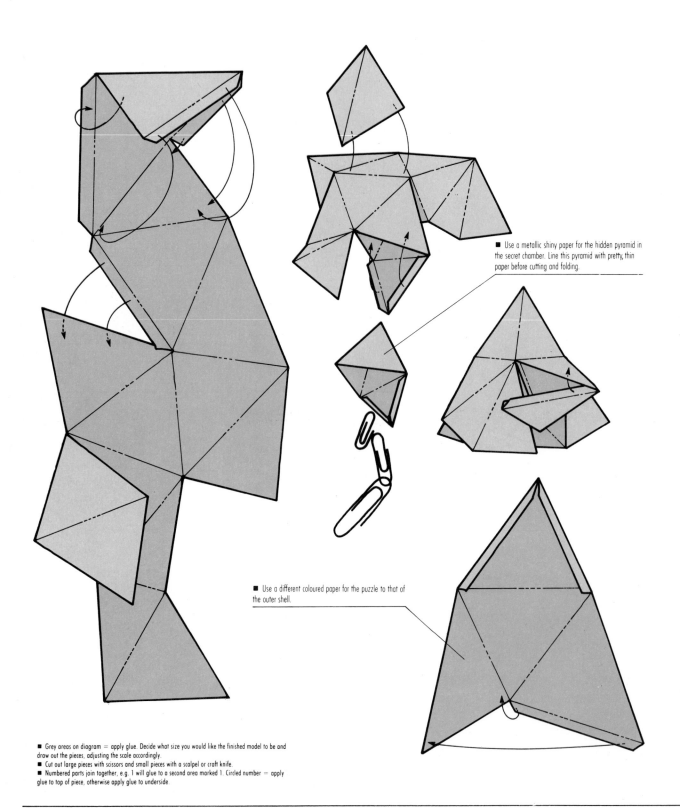

■ Use a metallic shiny paper for the hidden pyramid in the secret chamber. Line this pyramid with pretty, thin paper before cutting and folding.

■ Use a different coloured paper for the puzzle to that of the outer shell.

■ Grey areas on diagram = apply glue. Decide what size you would like the finished model to be and draw out the pieces, adjusting the scale accordingly.
■ Cut out large pieces with scissors and small pieces with a scalpel or craft knife.
■ Numbered parts join together, e.g. 1 will glue to a second area marked 1. Circled number = apply glue to top of piece, otherwise apply glue to underside.

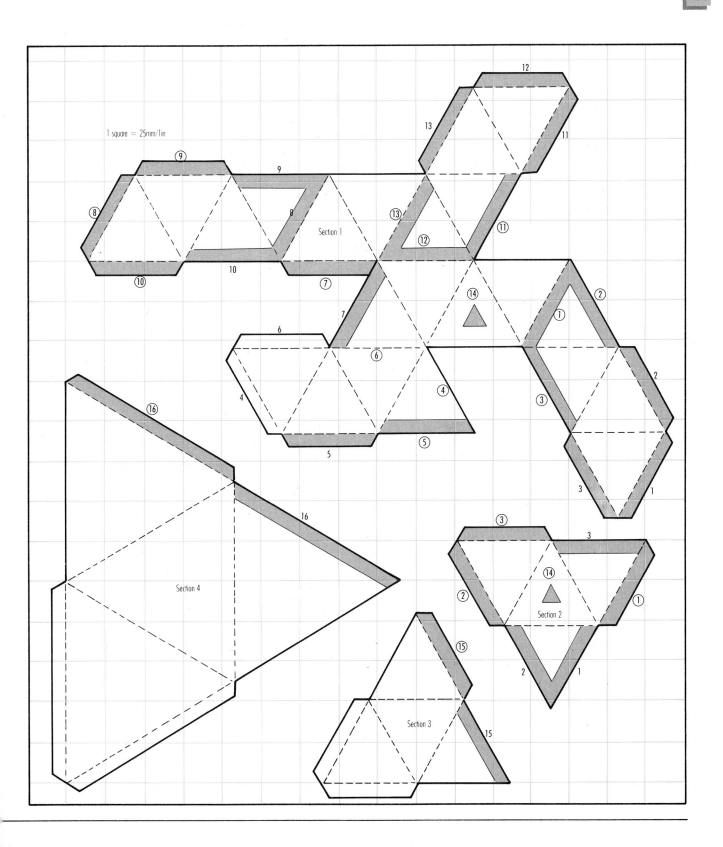

1 square = 25mm/1in

Section 1

Section 2

Section 3

Section 4

CRYING WOLF

The grid measurement provided creates a ferocious wolf just the right size to spit tissues at you from a cube-shaped 'Boutique' style tissue box. The instructions are given for one side of the head only for simplicity. Repeat each instruction in an identical manner for the opposite side of the head.

1 Cut out and score all the pieces that form the head, the eyes and fangs.

2 Glue, on section 1, 1 to **1**, 2 to **2**, 3 to **3**, 4 to **4** and 5 to **5**. Don't forget to make the same joins on both sides of the head. Glue 6 to 6 by folding the nose into the head. This is the trickiest bit in the entire book so take your time and think about it, it *is* possible.

3 Join 7 to the opposite half of the lower jaw.

4 Join 8 to **8**.

5 Curve **9** under the nose and glue it to its opposite number on the other side of the head.

6 Take section 2 and insert it into 1 by gluing 10 to **10**, 11 to **11**, 12 to **12** and 13 to **13**. Carry this out on the inverse side of the head.

7 Join section 3 by gluing 14 to **14**.

8 Slip the wolf's dentures into place and hold firm with a drop of glue.

9 Before cutting out, line each ear with pink paper. Attach each ear by gluing 15 to **15** and 16 to **16**.

10 Turn to the body. Glue 17 to **17** and 18 to **18**. After this glue 19 to **19** and 20 to **20**.

11 On section 2 glue 21 to **21** and 22 to **22**.

12 Glue section 2 to section 1 by joining 23 to **23** and 24 to **24**.

13 Build the tissue spout by sticking 25 to **25** and then tabs 26 to **26**.

14 Insert the spout into the back of the wolf's head by gluing tabs 27 inside the jaw.

15 Attach the head to the body by gluing 28 to **28**, and then cut out the eyes and score them. Glue tabs 30 to **30**, making sure the 'reverse cone' of the eyes works as in the photo, and glue 31 to **31** and 32 to **32** on the head.

1 Thread a tissue through the spout into the mouth.

2 As you do this draw the open end of the tissue spout towards the box until you are able to insert it into the box. The rim will fit completely within the tissue box.

3 The body wraps around the box until the holes 29 coincide. From these holes the wolf may be hung gargoyle-like from a wall. The tissues will follow one after the other from the mouth as if they were being plucked conventionally from the open box.

YOU WILL NEED:
- ☐ Scalpel or modelling knife
- ☐ Scissors
- ☐ Impact adhesive
- ☐ 2 A2 sheets of 200gsm brown paper
- ☐ 1 A4 sheet of 80gsm pink paper
- ☐ Some scraps of cream paper for the fangs
- ☐ Paint to tint the eyes

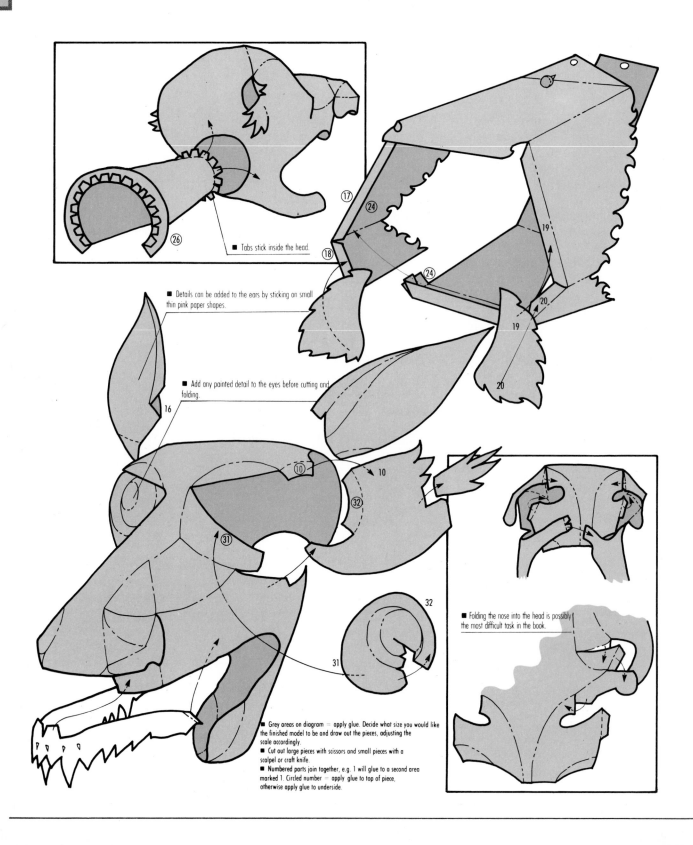

■ Tabs stick inside the head.

■ Details can be added to the ears by sticking on small thin pink paper shapes.

■ Add any painted detail to the eyes before cutting and folding.

■ Folding the nose into the head is possibly the most difficult task in the book.

■ Grey areas on diagram = apply glue. Decide what size you would like the finished model to be and draw out the pieces, adjusting the scale accordingly.
■ Cut out large pieces with scissors and small pieces with a scalpel or craft knife.
■ Numbered parts join together, e.g. 1 will glue to a second area marked 1. Circled number = apply glue to top of piece, otherwise apply glue to underside.

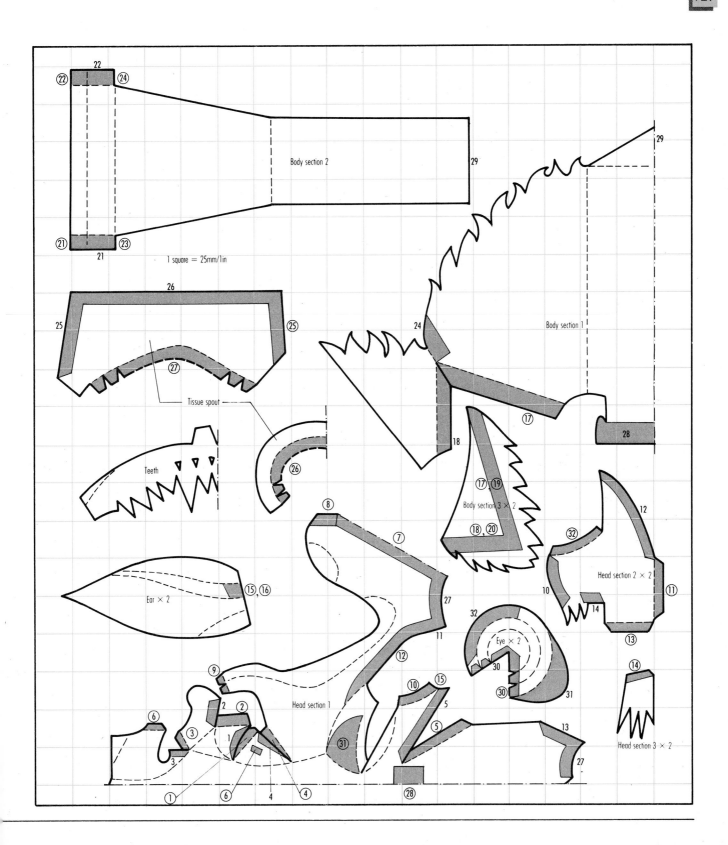

Body section 2

1 square = 25mm/1in

Body section 1

Tissue spout

Teeth

Ear × 2

Head section 1

Body section 3 × 2

Head section 2 × 2

Eye × 2

Head section 3 × 2

PEN PUSHER

The grid measurement provided will build an engine 400mm/15¾in long.

1 Cut out the fire box. This is just a modified box shape so it is an easy affair to glue 1 to **1**, 2 to **2** etc through to 10 to **10**. Fold around the coal box holder and secure 11 to **11**.

2 Cut out the three boiler sections from green paper. Some black and gold paper may be added for decorative detail, this is accomplished most easily before folding the boiler sections. Gently roll section 1 to form a tube then apply glue to tabs 12 on piece 2 and stick into place.

3 In the same way secure piece 3 into position 13 to **13**, making sure that the arrow points upwards (12 o'clock) and finally glue 14 to **14**. Care should be taken throughout this stage.

4 Apply glue to tabs 15 on the fire box and push the boiler through these up to the line indicated on the plan.

YOU WILL NEED:
- ☐ Scalpel or modelling knife
- ☐ Scissors
- ☐ Impact adhesive
- ☐ 1 SRA2 sheet of 250gsm black paper (preferably shiny)
- ☐ 1 SRA2 sheet of 200gsm green shiny paper
- ☐ 1 SRA2 sheet of 200gsm red paper
- ☐ 1 SRA2 sheet of 200gsm silver or grey shiny paper
- ☐ Offcuts of silver foil and gold paper
- ☐ 2 drinking straws

5 Cut the chimney from black paper. Glue 16 to **16**. Spread the glue on the tabs in the boiler and slip the chimney into the hole.

6 Cut out the pieces to make one back wheel (12 spokes, one hub, one rim, one back and a 'tread' strip). One at a time, glue the spokes into position on the wheel back. Note which end must face out from

the wheel 17 to **17**. When all the spokes are in position take the tread strip and, after folding all tabs and applying glue to the outer side, pull it around tightly and glue 18 to **18**. The tabs 19 must face upwards. Fold tabs 19 inwards, apply glue to the upper surface and glue the rim on top. To provide strength also apply glue to the area on the spokes that

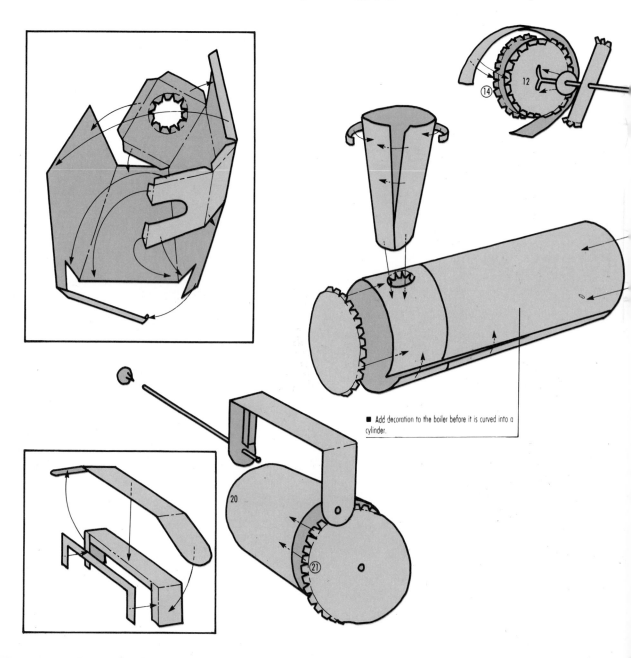

■ Add decoration to the boiler before it is curved into a cylinder.

will be covered by the rim.

7 Take a drinking straw, cut it to 175mm/6⅞in and split both ends. With two small pieces of tape, secure one end of the straw to the inside centre of the wheel hub in such a way that the straw juts out from the centre of the hub. Apply plenty of glue to the inside of the hub. Thread the unattached end of the straw through the X-shaped incision in the centre of the wheel back, until the hub becomes stuck to the spokes in the centre of the wheel.

8 Make up a second wheel by following instruction 6, only do not attach the hub yet.

9 Take the wheel and drinking straw axle and thread the axle through the fire box, through the X-shaped

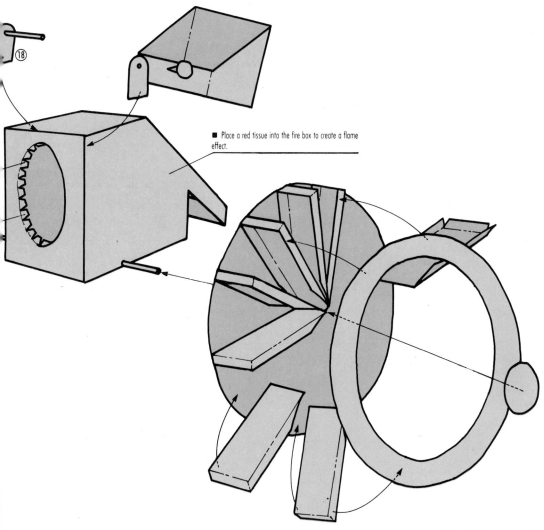

■ Place a red tissue into the fire box to create a flame effect.

■ Grey areas on diagram apply glue. Decide what size you would like the finished model to be and draw out the pieces, adjusting the scale accordingly
■ Cut out large pieces with scissors and small pieces with a scalpel or craft knife
■ Numbered parts join together, e.g. 1 will glue to a second area marked 1. Circled number apply glue to top of piece, otherwise apply glue to underside

incision in the wheel back on the second wheel. Attach the divided end of the axle to the second wheel hub as before and glue the hub into position on the spokes of the second wheel.

10 Cut out the three pieces that form the roller. It is built like the boiler, so glue tabs 20 to **20** on the rim (piece 3). In the same way, glue tabs 21 to **21** and finally secure 22 to **22**.

11 Cut out the three pieces that form the roller arch. Fold pieces 1 and 2 along the dotted lines. Attach 1 to 2 by gluing 1 to **1**, 2 to **2**, 3 to **3** but make sure tabs 4, 5 and 6 are not glued down. Fold these tabs out and glue roller arch 3 in position 5 to **5**, 6 to **6** and 4 to **4**.

12 Stick the roller arch to the front of the boiler 7 to **7**.

13 Place the roller between the arms of the roller arch and thread a straw through the arch and roller so that it will roll freely. To prevent the axle from coming adrift make up two roller securing pins **10A** to 10A and, with a spot of glue, slip one into each open end of the straw.

14 Cut out all the pieces that form the fly wheel. Back up the two fly wheels 12 to **12** and fold the tabs 13 and 14 in opposite directions. Secure the fly wheel rim onto these.

15 Take a drinking straw (cover it with coloured tape for decoration if you wish), and secure it into the middle in the same way as on to the wheel hubs — divide the end of the straw and make firm with two small pieces of tape. Spread glue on the fly wheel support ring and thread the wheel down over the fly wheel axle onto the join. Apply pressure to make firm. Thread the axle support rim onto the axle, secure tabs 15 and 16 into the rim.

16 Stick the fly wheel supports onto the fire box 17 to **17** and 18 to **18**, thread the axle through the holes and make a pin identical to those for the roller and slip this into the open end of the axle.

17 Cut out the coal box. Glue 19 to **19**, 21 to **21**, 22 to **22** and 20 to **20**. Slip the completed coal box into the holder at the back of the fire box.

To enhance the completed model, add a small gold paper disc to the centre of each back wheel, and attach gold trimming to the chimney. Pens and pencils may be kept in the holes cut into the upper surface of the fire box, and when inserted into the wheels they will drive the engine along.

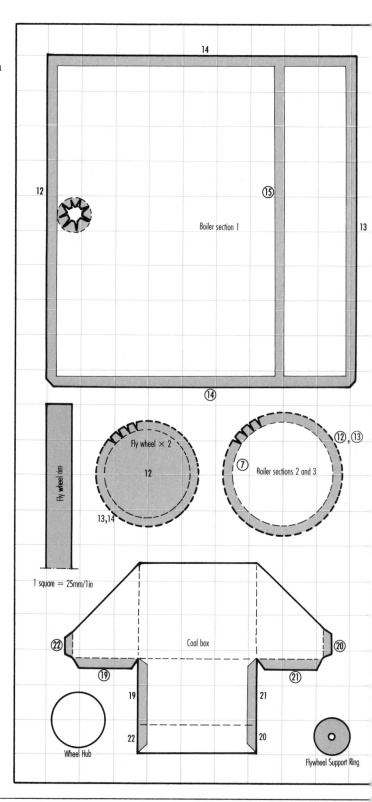

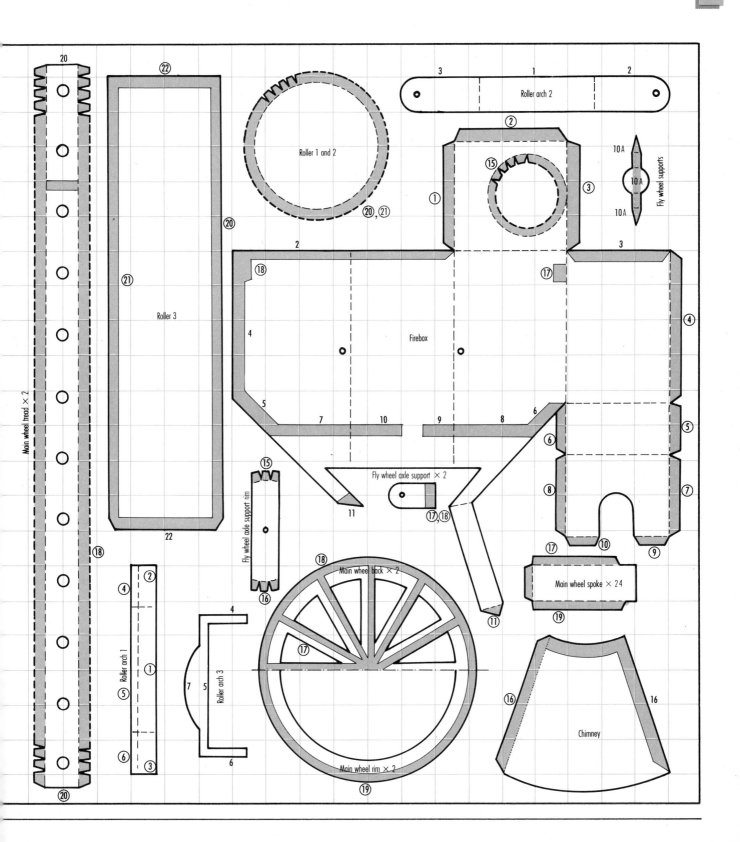

PEN-DRIVEN PADDLE STEAMER

The grid measurement provided builds a paddle steamer 482mm/19in long.

1 Cut out the two main deck pieces. Notice the example of deck wall strip shown. The two main decks must be joined by gluing the wall strip around the perimeter of one deck, and also around the paddle hole, then the second main deck piece glued on top to give one single piece with increased thickness and rigidity.

To provide extra strength it is helpful if another section of wall strip is glued inside the deck in a zig-zag pattern (refer to the illustration for guidance).

2 Working in an identical manner assemble the 'upper front deck' and the 'upper rear deck'. In each case cut out two deck pieces and join them by sandwiching a wall strip between them. All of this modelling is best done with the thick, black paper.

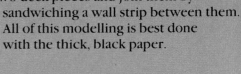

3 Cut out the two paddle wheels and 19 paddle blades from white paper. To begin constructing the paddle, stick four blades into position at each quarter turn of one wheel, then lower the second wheel into position on top of the four paddles. One by one each of the remaining paddles can now be glued into position inside the paddle 1 to **1**. Take time over this section as the more accurately positioned the paddles, the better the complete model will work.

4 Cut out the four bell-shaped paddle supports and two paddle support arches (from white paper). Pair off the paddle supports by backing them up and gluing together 2 to **2**. Make sure that all the tabs remain free.

5 Take the paddle support arches and glue them into position around each support 3 to **3**.

6 Glue the completed supports on each side of the paddle hole in the main deck.

7 Insert the paddle in between the two supports and thread a drinking straw through the aligned holes.

YOU WILL NEED:
- ☐ Scalpel or modelling knife
- ☐ Scissors
- ☐ Impact adhesive
- ☐ 3 SRA2 sheets of 200gsm white paper
- ☐ 2 SRA2 sheets of 400gsm black paper
- ☐ 3 A4 sheets of tissue paper in assorted colours
- ☐ Coloured papers, paints and pens for decoration
- ☐ 1 drinking straw
- ☐ A length of white cotton

Cut the excess length of the straw off and secure by slipping the sharp end of a paddle pin into each open end of the straw.

8 Before cutting out each of the cabin sections from the white paper line them with coloured tissue paper. Cut out front lower cabins. Glue 4 to 4 and then glue the entire piece into place on the main deck 5 to **5**.

9 Glue the front upper platform on top of this, ensuring that the rear section does not interfere with the free movement of the paddle.

10 Cut out rear lower cabins from white paper. Glue 4 to 4 then position and glue onto the main deck 6 to **6**.

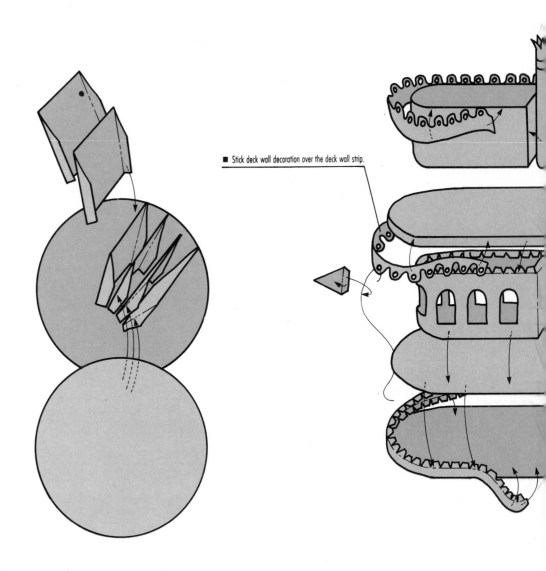

■ Stick deck wall decoration over the deck wall strip.

11 Glue the rear platform on top, again making sure that it does not restrict the paddle's movement.
12 Cut out the front upper cabins, glue 7 to **7**. Stick this onto the front upper deck 8 to **8**.
13 Carrying on in the same way, cut out the back upper cabins, glue 9 to **9**. Then glue the piece onto the rear platform 10 to **10**.
14 Cut out and glue into position the upper front platform 11 to **11**.
15 Cut out the pencil chute support, glue 12 to **12**. Glue on the upper platform 13 to **13**, 14 to **14**, 15 to **15**, 16 to **16**. Cut out the chute itself and glue tabs 15A to **15A**.

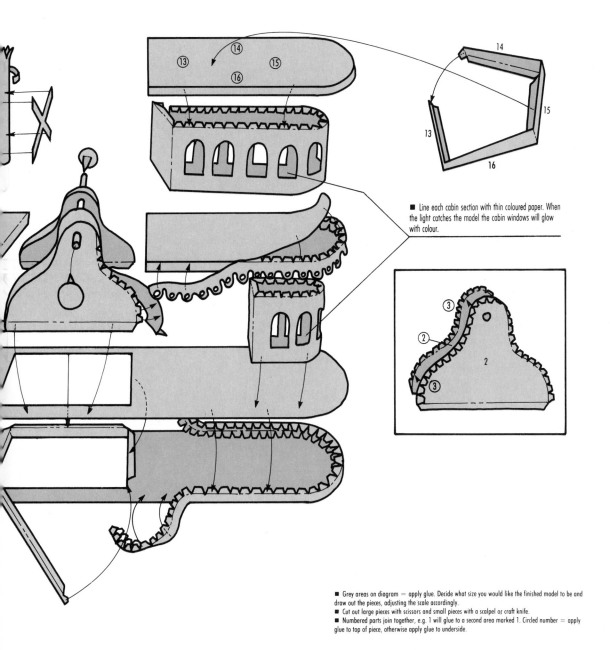

■ Line each cabin section with thin coloured paper. When the light catches the model the cabin windows will glow with colour.

■ Grey areas on diagram = apply glue. Decide what size you would like the finished model to be and draw out the pieces, adjusting the scale accordingly.
■ Cut out large pieces with scissors and small pieces with a scalpel or craft knife.
■ Numbered parts join together, e.g. 1 will glue to a second area marked 1. Circled number = apply glue to top of piece, otherwise apply glue to underside.

16 To make the chimneys, cut out the two pieces and, one at a time, wrap them around a pencil, then glue 17 to **17** to secure them. Gently splay out the spiked top. Glue into position against the cabin wall 18 to **18**. Cut out and glue the chimney struts to the chimneys.
17 To enhance the model with a little decoration, cut

out several strips of platform wall decoration and line each platform with it.
18 Thread a piece of cotton through a central hole in the upper platform wall decoration and secure both ends underneath the bottom main deck. Cut out a triangular flag shape and attach to the cotton by

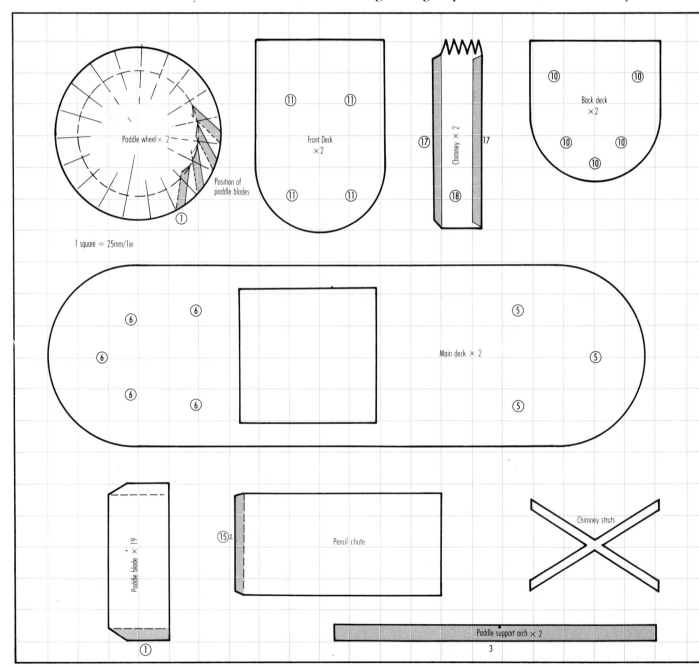

Paddle wheel × 2

Position of paddle blades

①

1 square = 25mm/1in

Front Deck ×2

⑪   ⑪

⑪   ⑪

Chimney × 2

⑰   17

⑱

Back deck ×2

⑩   ⑩

⑩   ⑩

⑩

⑥   ⑥

⑥

⑥

⑥

Main deck × 2

⑤

⑤

⑤

Paddle blade × 19

①

⑮A

Pencil chute

Chimney struts

Paddle support arch × 2

3

turning over a small flap and gluing it around the thread. Repeat this process for the other end of the paddle steamer.

To drive the paddle, release pens or pencils one by one down the pencil shute. These will drop onto each paddle blade and rotate the wheel before sliding out and rolling along the main deck.

Rubber bands, rolls of sticky tape, scissors, staples, paperclips and the other bits and pieces which litter desk-tops can be kept in the steamer's various holds. Pencils and pens can be slotted onto the platform or poked into the two chimneys.

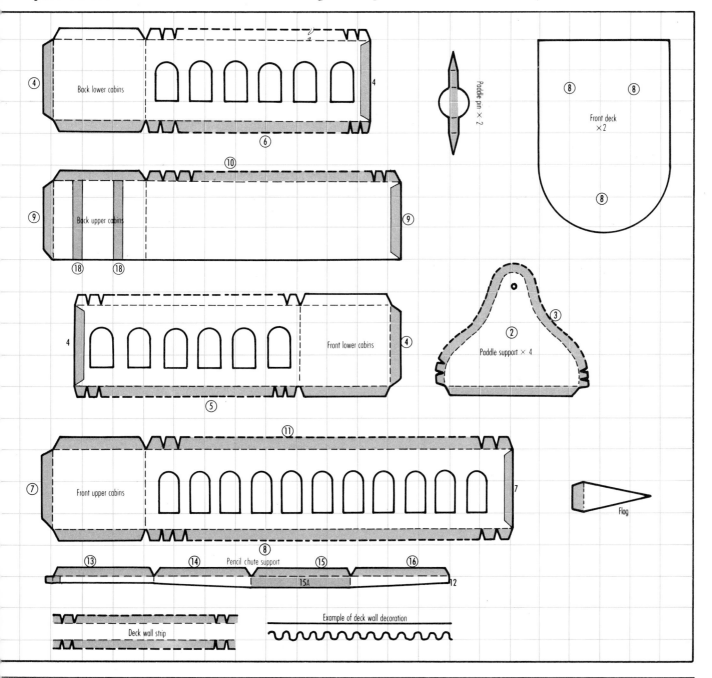

Back lower cabins

Back upper cabins

Front lower cabins

Front upper cabins

Paddle pin × 2

Front deck ×2

Paddle support × 4

Flag

Pencil chute support

15A

Deck wall strip

Example of deck wall decoration

INDEX